FAMILY SECRETS

Jean-Yves Soucy
with Annette,
Cécile & Yvonne Dionne

Translated by Käthe Roth

Stoddart

Published in 1996 by
Stoddart Publishing Co. Limited
34 Lesmill Road
Toronto, Canada
M3B 2T6
Tel. (416) 445-3333
Fax (416) 445-5967

Published by arrangement with Les Éditions Libre Expression
2016 rue Saint-Hubert
Montreal, Quebec H2L 3Z5

Stoddart Books are available for bulk purchase for sales promotions,
premiums, fundraising, and seminars. For details, contact the
Special Sales Department at the above address.

Canadian Cataloguing in Publication Data
Soucy, Jean-Yves, 1945–
Family secrets

Translation of: Secrets de famille.
ISBN 0-7737-5803-8

1. Dionne quintuplets.   2. Dionne quintuplets – Family relationships.
I. Title.
CT9998.D5S6813 1996   920.0713   C95-933298-7

Cover Design: the boy 100 & Tannice Goddard
Text Design: Tannice Goddard
Printed and bound in Canada

*Stoddart Publishing gratefully acknowledges the support
of the Canada Council, the Ontario Ministry of Citizenship,
Culture and Recreation, Ontario Arts Council, and
Ontario Publishing Centre in the development of
writing and publishing in Canada.*

To the memory of
Émilie and Marie

To the fond memory of
Émilie and Marie, to my family,
to all my beloved descendants.

For a very long time, I have racked my brains trying to understand why in my family there were so many fights, so much heartbreak, and so much distance and coldness. I have long sought the reasons for the hate and vengeance that were woven through my childhood and adolescence.

When I was just eight years old (though I felt much older), I unconsciously gathered feelings of guilt and world-weariness that stunted both my emotional and my physical growth.

There was a total lack of communication in our home, which didn't make things any easier. Money, family rights, language, religion, politics — all of these issues provoked arguments and left a legacy of bitterness. I ached to know why my family was so unhappy. Only little by little did I figure out that the source of all these miseries was my own birth, which was said to be extraordinary, even miraculous — a label that marked me to the depths of my soul!

How painful it was to realize that I had no ties with the other members of my family, all of whom suffered their own private torments. In a sense, the others were completely overshadowed by the simultaneous birth of five babies among them. It goes without saying that moments of peace and pleasure were few and fleeting.

Of course, I wish with all my heart to make amends with you, the members of my family with whom I lived in the "big house." But, with the passage of time, I have finally understood that since I had no responsibility for my own birth, I cannot accept guilt for being alive. In fact, I am owed forgiveness for having been burdened with so much misery and responsibility. However, I can imagine how wounded you were by this event, which "poisoned" your life. Please believe that I have the greatest respect for each and every one of you.

However, I am very touched when I realize that for a completely different group of people, I am considered a source of love, hope, and courage. It comforts me to know that, through the media, we have opened up a channel of communication. I deplore the fact that some people think I confuse adoration and admiration with love. In all my life, I never wanted to be adored and admired.

To all "multiples" now living or yet to come: as the "grand old lady," I feel a natural connection to and a very tender regard for you. I feel that I am somehow with you and that a thread, as tenuous and mysterious as it may seem to you, exists between us and will always be there. I am with you, and I love you. May your heavenly protectors guard, guide, and protect you. Believe in their love.

I would like to thank Jean-Yves for his tact and respect during our interviews, and for his sensitive and subtle intelligence. It was pleasant and interesting to see how gently our partnership grew.

My thanks go to all those who held out a hand to me, supported me, and helped me see the light at the end of the long tunnel. Because of you, I learned to know and value myself — to love myself. By teaching me not to remain a "victim" and by standing behind me through all the new experiences — the abundance of lessons that life hands out — you have contributed to my transformation from a caterpillar to a butterfly. I hope that my recognition will reflect divine strength upon you.

I can never sufficiently thank God, who grants the impossible, for the blessing of having served as a "channel" to my dear children, whom I love with all my heart.

Émilie, Marie, Annette, and Yvonne, my heart will always be with you, to the end of time. I thank the Almighty for having lived through this experience with you.

Humbly and sincerely,

Cécile Dionne, individual

My wish is for multiple births
to take place in joy and peace
and with a warm welcome.
May the Heavenly Star protect
and guide them in their steps.
To you, my pledge of total love.

Annette Dionne

As a dedication, I offer the words
of Brother Roger de Taizé,
written to be used by everyone
in his or her personal life.
When our lives are perturbed
or thrown into upheaval,
there is a Presence out there to say to us:
"When you find that you are tried most sorely,
I will always be there beneath your despair.
And remember, I am also in the depths
of most radiant hope."

Yvonne Dionne

1

What's going to happen to us?

Yvonne started. Had one of her sisters spoken these words, or had she thought them? It was hard to tell.

Her forehead pressed against the window, the nine-year-old looked out at the dismal countryside in the dull light of a late-November afternoon. She didn't notice the rust-colored fields or the spruce trees that seemed to be fading from green to gray. What she was staring at was the large house made of ochre bricks set slightly back from the other side of the road: her parents' new home. She had never lived with her parents. They were almost strangers — strangers whom she had learned to mistrust over the last few years. She had yet to learn how to love them.

Yvonne clutched her big Shirley Temple doll tighter. It was her most prized possession. Tears came to her eyes, but she blinked them back so that the others, who were just as sad as she was, wouldn't see.

She turned toward her sisters. Really, she wondered for the thousandth time, how could people mix them up?

Each one was so different from the others, and they tried so hard to be unique! Of course, they had the same round faces, brown eyes, thick shoulder-length hair, and dimples in their cheeks when they smiled. Of course, they were often made to wear the same dresses, and they were all rather small for their age. Nevertheless, a thousand little details told them apart. You had to look at each one individually, rather than taking them all in at once, to see the differences. And no one did that. They weren't allowed to be Yvonne, Marie, Annette, Émilie, and Cécile — instead they were "*les petites*," "the little girls," the "quints."

Sitting on the floor in a corner, apart from the others, as she often was, Cécile rocked a doll just like Yvonne's. She looked more withdrawn and pensive than usual. She raised her head and her eyes met Yvonne's; they recognized the distress in each other's face. There was no need to speak. Yvonne wanted to reassure Cécile, but it was a lost cause; their world was crumbling, and they were all wondering anxiously what would become of them.

In the center of the empty room that had been their playroom for almost ten years, Marie tried to cheer her sisters up by telling the story of the time when Émilie had pulled off Monseigneur Nelligan's skullcap and they had each tried it on. Her audience, however, remained unmoved, and her laugh rang false. Sometimes left out because she was smaller and more delicate than the others, Marie often resorted to clowning to get their attention. Today, her antics weren't working.

Annette's expression was glum and a little stubborn. She was filled with an intense feeling of revolt. They had not been consulted about this move. They were never asked how they felt about anything, so why should things change now? They would have to give in and, as always, make believe.

Like the others, Émilie paid no attention to Marie. No longer the playful tomboy, she was now a heartsick little girl. She had been silently repeating the same prayer for the last half hour, praying that this was all just a bad dream, that when she woke up life would be as it had been, full of games, laughter, and the attention of devoted nurses — an existence protected by two chain-link fences and armed guards. People saw it as a prison, but it was the only world that Émilie and her sisters had ever known, and they had always been happy under the watchful eyes of their guardians. But it was useless to dream: this evening they would be sleeping in the big brick house, with their "family." Émilie burst into tears, and Yvonne rushed over to comfort her. Soon, they were all sniffling — even Annette, who liked to pretend she was tough.

In "The Dafoe Hospital and Nursery," as a plaque near the entrance called it, the five most famous children in the world wept bitterly. They had been in three feature films and dozens of shorts, and thousands of photographs of them had appeared in newspapers all over the world the day they were born, May 28, 1934. Their likenesses had been used to advertise hundreds of products. In many languages, the word "quintuplet" had been invented to describe them. Over almost a decade, three million visitors had come to Callander and Corbeil, small towns near the Dionne farm in Northern Ontario, to catch a glimpse of them. Were they teething? Did they have a cold? Such events made headlines all over North America.

Today, they were simply five little girls whose future was full of uncertainty. They had only a vague idea of the

3

battle their father had waged for years to get them back, and they were unaware that a bank account in their names contained almost a million dollars. Today, November 17, 1943, the newspapers were trumpeting the long-awaited reunion of the Dionne quintuplets with their family, but it was the saddest day of their short lives.

They heard their father's footsteps in the hall. The five girls exchanged uneasy glances and, in a single spontaneous movement, each held her Shirley Temple doll tighter to her chest.

• • •

Suitcases in right hand, dolls clutched in left arm, the Dionne quints followed their father as he strode swiftly across the wet grass. Leaving the hospital did not mean leaving the fences topped with barbed wire: the new house was surrounded by a chain-link fence that abutted the one around the quints' home, and a gate provided access back and forth. For the first time, Émilie found these fences sinister and forbidding. She looked toward her sisters for solace, but all of them had their eyes riveted to the ground.

Oliva Dionne said not a word during the short walk. When they got to the big brick house, instead of going in the front entrance he used the service door off the kitchen. Her heart pounding, Yvonne was the first to follow her father inside. She was no less scared than her sisters, but her sense of obligation toward them gave her courage. She was, they said, the first of the five to be born, and she often played a maternal, protective role.

The warm kitchen provided a cheery contrast to the nippy night air, and the aroma of stew gave the room a familiar feeling. For a moment, Émilie let herself believe that it canceled out the evil omen of the fences, but the sight of her mother before the steaming pots quickly snuffed out all hope. In her mind's eye, she saw her mother, her eyes wide, her mouth twisted into a grimace, yelling, "You're just a crazy little girl! A crazy little girl who should be locked up!"

Émilie had been five years old. Under the watchful eye of the nurse, Miss Corriveau, she'd been playing with her sisters in the playground surrounded by the observation gallery. Simone and Lucie, their older sisters, had joined them. Suddenly, a cry rose above the dull murmur of the onlookers' laughs and whispers.

"Simone! Lucie! Come here!"

Elzire Dionne burst into the playground. She was in a bad mood, and Simone and Lucie went to her right away. Miss Corriveau suggested that the quints go and say hello to their mother, but they hung back. Yvonne said, "We don't want to. Mom says mean things to us."

"She says that you and Miss Michaud and Miss O'Shaughnessy and Dr. Dafoe are nasty, not nice, and that we shouldn't listen to you," added Cécile, tears in her eyes. "She says we should only listen to her and our teacher, Miss Vézina."

"Come over here and see me!" Elzire called in a harsh, unfriendly voice.

Only Annette went. Yvonne and Cécile stayed beside the nurse, while Émilie and Marie stopped halfway and would go no farther, despite their mother's repeated exhortations.

Angrily, Elzire shouted at Marie, "You're dirty and you play with your bum! You make the Baby Jesus cry!"

To Émilie, she yelled, "You're a crazy little girl. Completely crazy!"

5

Marie and Émilie, in tears, ran to Louise Corriveau and hid behind her skirt. Elzire came after them, gesticulating. She, too, was crying, and she threatened loudly, between sobs, "You just wait! I'm going to tell your father you don't want to see me. And when I tell him, he won't be happy!"

She stopped three steps from Miss Corriveau, fists clenched, her face scarlet. "It's your fault!" she shrieked. "You're the devil in the flesh! You don't love my girls, you just work here for the money! You're bringing them up wrong! All you want is to take them away from me!"

Miss Corriveau retorted, sharply, "Stop making a spectacle of yourself. It's not you that people come to see!"

"Do you think you can shut me up? People have to know what you're putting me through, you and the others. You're stealing my children! You're putting them on display like animals in a cage!"

She turned toward the quints. "Your father doesn't want you to play here, in front of all those people. It's not normal! And I don't want you to, either."

Miss Corriveau gathered the children and nudged them toward the door.

"We're going inside."

The girls hurried into the hospital, eager to escape the terrifying scene. Their mother walked behind them, calling them heartless and ungrateful, threatening to tell all to their father, who, she assured them, would be furious.

Like Annette, Cécile, Yvonne, and Marie, Émilie had been completely heartsick. Was her mother right to be angry at Miss Corriveau? And above all, why was she being so spiteful to her own daughters? There were so many things that they didn't understand about the world of adults, and it hurt them to have their happiness so often disrupted by quarrels between grown-ups. They felt torn. On one side were their parents, whom they were supposed to love, and their teacher, whom they had to obey; on the other side were Dr. Dafoe, whom they trusted, and the nurses, whom they loved. Often, they didn't know what to think.

It had been four years since their mother had said those words in the playground of the hospital, but Émilie couldn't forget them. It was as though they were an eternal judgment on her.

"The little girls are here," Oliva announced as he left the kitchen.

In the warm kitchen, Émilie shivered as her mother spun around with a nimbleness that belied her obesity. Elzire's small, bright eyes moved from girl to girl, and a smile briefly lit up her features. In spite of her thirty-four years and nine pregnancies, her face had not lost its youthful appearance.

"Good evening, Mom," said the quints in unison, addressing Elzire in English, as the other children did.

"Supper will be ready soon," answered their mother, absently.

Preoccupied with her cooking, Elzire shouted toward the hall, "Simone! Lucie!"

The girls came slowly from the dining room into the kitchen.

"Have you finished setting the table? Show the little girls around the house."

Elzire turned back to her pots, her unflattering tent of a dress, mauve with yellow flowers, rustling around her more than ample figure.

Simone, thirteen, stared rudely at the five little girls, who were still clutching their suitcases and dolls. She felt that, by the simple fact of their existence, the quints had

7

stolen her childhood away. Even though they had never lived with the family, they were the only subject of conversation. To hear her parents talk, they would never be happy until the "little girls" came home! When she had played with them in the hospital playground from time to time, she had no sense that these were her sisters; they seemed more like strangers.

"Come on."

The five little girls trailed along behind Simone, and Lucie brought up the rear. Pointing to closed doors, Simone announced, "The boys' rooms . . . the leather den . . . the old man's private office . . . the damn cow's sewing room . . ."

The quints were shocked to hear such terms used to describe their parents, and they exchanged surprised glances. But their sisters had already led them into the immense dining room, divided by an archway.

"This side," Simone said scathingly, "is for our family. The other side is for your family."

The newcomers didn't flinch at this blow, but their worst fears had been confirmed.

As the tour continued, they didn't dare ask where they were to put their suitcases and coats. The rooms smelled of fresh paint and all the furniture was brand new. The house seemed cold, unlived in. Too big. In the living room, which stretched nearly a full thirty feet, a painting of the quints at age five hung over the fireplace.

"It doesn't look much like you. The painter had a good imagination." Lucie's tone was scornful and superior.

Although her father liked to introduce her as the "sixth quintuplet," Lucie felt that she was infinitely prettier and more charming than her famous sisters, who were only eleven months younger than she was. Once they had dressed her up just like the quints for a photograph, but her curly brown hair, slender figure, and fine features had made her stand out from the other five.

Yvonne could easily hear the animosity in Lucie's voice, and she detected a glint of sarcasm in the eyes that scrutinized her from head to toe. The blood rose to her cheeks, but at the last second she restrained herself from retorting and made believe that she had heard nothing. Making believe, as they had always been taught. Like the time they had made believe it was Christmas and unwrapped their gifts for the camera, celebrating the holidays two weeks before everyone else so that the photographs and films could come out on time.

When they found themselves at the foot of the imposing staircase rising from the entrance hall, Simone said to Lucie, "Show them their rooms."

The upper floor, divided lengthwise by a hallway, had eight bedrooms and five bathrooms. The quints were stunned to learn that from now on they wouldn't be sleeping together in one room, as they had since birth. The only time they had been separated for an entire night was when they were five and taking a special train to Toronto to meet the King and Queen of England. Two to a room? There were five of them; someone would have to be alone.

Seeing their dejection, Lucie couldn't help smiling. She pointed to Yvonne and Émilie. "The green room. Mom decided."

Émilie was relieved that she would be with Yvonne. The other three waited anxiously.

"The yellow room . . ." Lucie began, drawing things out. Then, after a moment of suspense, she pointed to Cécile and Annette.

Marie's face fell: she would be sharing the pink room with Lucie.

"I don't like this any better than you do," Lucie said to her coldly.

Cécile found it cruel that it was the frailest of the quints who would be separated from the others. As was her habit, she tried to sacrifice herself for her sisters.

"Why don't I take the room with you?" she proposed to Lucie. This would mean that Marie could be with Annette.

After hesitating a moment, Lucie shrugged. "Go complain to the fat cow if you're not happy."

This idea didn't appeal to Cécile. Her intuition told her that it would be better not to make a fuss, especially on their first day in the house. She had studied her family a bit in the three years since their contact had become more frequent, and she knew that Lucie had a lot of influence with her parents. "What if you asked her?" she suggested.

"No way! Everybody minds their own business here!" Lucie retorted in English. With this, she turned on her heel and quickly walked away. She was so unpredictable that they never knew what to expect from her.

A shout from downstairs announced that dinner was served. The quints dropped their belongings in their rooms, pulled off their coats, and ran downstairs.

• • •

The table, large enough for sixteen places, was almost full. Around Elzire and Oliva, their twelve children sat stiffly in their chairs. For Oliva, it was a moment of triumph, the culmination of nine years of struggle. In his joy, he didn't notice the tension that hung over the dining room: the quints were self-conscious, and the other children were upset by the presence of these intruders. Elzire served the meal, and each plate passed was a reminder that her family had just grown from nine to fourteen. She had never seen the return of the quints in this light, nor had she considered how much work would go into the upkeep of a nineteen-room house!

Sitting between Armand, already a young man of seventeen, and Rachel, who was fifteen, Yvonne suddenly felt very strange, as if she had already lived through this supper somewhere else. Perhaps it reminded her of the many Sundays over the last two years when she and the other quints had eaten with the rest of the family in their old gray clapboard house — the house where the "miracle of Corbeil" had taken place. The decor was different here — more luxurious — but Yvonne sensed the same curiosity in the eyes of her brothers and sisters, and the same lack of sympathy. It was as if she were an exotic animal.

In the old house, the quints had sat at one end of the table; together, it seemed easier to endure the stares of the others. Today, they were scattered among the other members of the family. Marie was to Yvonne's right, on the other side of Rachel, and Lucie and Roger were between her and their father. Facing her, Serge, Laurent, and Simone were sitting between Cécile, Émilie, and Annette.

Separated for sleeping, separated for eating, Yvonne thought, her heart heavy. The closeness between her and her sisters would no longer be allowed. Part of their life was truly coming to a close. When she made eye contact with the others, Yvonne saw the same thoughts. And yet, they mustn't let themselves dread the worst. After all, it was just the first night, the first meal after the reunion. It made sense that everyone would be uneasy, a little awkward. Things would work out.

Yvonne looked for reasons to rejoice. The fine white tablecloth, her father's three-piece suit and tie — weren't they intended to create an atmosphere of celebration and honor for their arrival? True, they had not come in through the front door, and no one had wished them welcome. But a reunion like this wasn't something that happened every day, so it wasn't surprising that no one knew how to act.

The meal proceeded in silence. The only sounds were forks scraping against plates and curt requests: "Butter!" or "Salt!" Yvonne was accustomed to pleasant meals, full of animated conversation with the nurses — exactly the opposite of the stultifying atmosphere that reigned here.

Oliva Dionne pushed his plate away and used a finger-nail to dislodge a bit of meat from between his teeth. He cleared his throat to get everyone's attention.

"Now, we're one big family. No more divisions." He was unsure of himself at first, but his voice grew firmer as he continued. "You little girls, you have to stop seeing yourselves as quintuplets. Look how we've seated you at the table: here, each of you is one child among twelve. Not one among five, one among twelve."

After glancing at Elzire, who got up and went to stand beside him, he concluded, "I've always wanted all my children to be treated the same."

As she weighed the meaning of her father's words, Yvonne noticed that her glass was chipped and a tine in her fork was bent. Those of her immediate neighbors were intact. As Yvonne craned her neck to check the state of her sisters' place settings, Armand noticed what

12

she was doing and asked, sharply, "Is something bothering you?"

"No," she replied quickly.

She lowered her head but raised it again just as quickly
when she heard her mother's voice.

"Sit up straight!" Elzire ordered, poking her index
finger between Marie's shoulder blades. "Do you want
your back to be as crooked as your eyes?"

This unkind jab at little Marie, who was slightly cross-
eyed, hurt Yvonne deeply.

A few minutes later, Elzire tapped Émilie's hand; she
was the only left-handed quint. "Use your right hand.
With all their 'scientific' child-rearing methods, the nurses
weren't able to cure you of that, eh? Too busy flirting
with the cops."

Her malicious tone reminded Yvonne of the scenes her
mother had made with the nurses, who were always so
nice. She tried not to think about it, but a cynical thought
popped into her mind: *So this is what it's like for all of us
to be treated the same!*

• • •

After the meal, the quints helped to clear the table. Since
it was their first day at home, their mother excused them
from drying the dishes, and they found themselves with
nothing to do. The rest of the family scattered throughout
the house without paying them any mind, so they went
upstairs and headed for the farthest room, Cécile and
Annette's. They sat on the two beds and said not a word,
each holding in her emotions so as not to demoralize the
others. They looked around the room, their only refuge in
this strange house. It was pretty, decorated with religious
pictures and statuettes, but impersonal. A door led to the

bathroom, which also served the neighboring bedroom.

"We could visit each other through there," said Émilie, who immediately regretted having reminded Marie that she would be isolated from the other four.

The door to the hallway suddenly opened to reveal Elzire, winded from having climbed the stairs so quickly.

"What are you doing here, all five of you? What kind of nonsense is this?"

Her tone made them feel as though they'd done something wrong.

"Didn't you hear your father? I don't want the five of you together any more, away from the others. All of you stay in your own rooms. And what's the idea of coming upstairs without saying good night? Come and give your father a kiss before you go to bed."

The quints docilely followed her down to the dining room, where Oliva was listening to the news about the war on the radio. At one end of the table, the five eldest children were playing cards. The little girls lined up, as they had done to shake a visitor's hand or kiss a bishop's ring. One by one, they planted a kiss on their father's cheek and said good night. Their heart wasn't in it; they were playing a role, one they had learned to play to perfection for the cameras.

Back in their room, Annette and Cécile unpacked their suitcases.

"Talk about a welcome!" Annette murmured sarcastically.

"It could have been worse."

"You think so?"

"Not so loud," Cécile said, with a finger to her lips. "You want them to hear us? We shouldn't go looking for trouble."

Annette sighed deeply. Of course, her sister was right.

14

After a few seconds, she whispered, "I didn't feel anything when I kissed Dad. Did you, Cécile?"

"Me neither."

"And yet, he's our father!"

"We'll have to learn to love our parents."

"How? Do you know, Cécile?"

Cécile hung a flannel nightgown in the wardrobe, then turned and looked at her sister for a moment before bowing her head.

"It'll come by itself, I imagine. In the meantime, make believe, as Miss Corriveau used to say."

Annette laughed under her breath, then whispered, "Anyway, I hope I don't end up loving them like Simone does. Did you hear what she called Mom and Dad?"

"It's terrible, I know, but it doesn't mean anything. Maybe it's just bad manners."

Annette shrugged. "You're always ready to think the best of people!" After a moment of reflection, she sighed. "Poor Marie, all alone in her corner."

• • •

Oliva stepped out onto the stoop to get a little air. On the other side of the road, the moon was shining on a shingled roof covered with a thin layer of frost: the little farmhouse, just like the others in the neighborhood, where all of his children had been born. The imposing home that he had just built, at a cost of $70,000, was, on the other hand, the largest and most luxurious in the region, almost a mansion. It was the best possible symbol of the path the family's life had taken in the last ten years.

When the quintuplets were born, Oliva was just another down-and-out farmer, a father of five, struggling to make ends meet during the Depression. He had mortgaged his farm so that he wouldn't have to depend on government handouts, and he was just beginning to think the worst was over when Elzire gave birth to five children all at once. It was a terrible blow! On top of that, hordes of reporters, photographers, and curious people came running, crying "Miracle!" Just one little item in the *Nugget*, the North Bay daily, and the news had traveled around the world in less than twenty-four hours.

Two days later, fifty reporters were knocking at the door, trampling the garden, peering through the windows. Oliva's father had to threaten them with a pitchfork to get them to back off. Day and night, they stood waiting on the road, and more kept arriving all the time. Oliva could no longer set foot outside his door without being besieged by them. Cameramen from Pathé and 20th-Century Fox stalked the place, filming everything: the house, the diapers on the clothesline. Dr. Dafoe, the doctor from Callander who had arrived at Elzire's bedside when two of the quints were already in a straw basket in front of the stove, was hogging the limelight. Making himself right at home, he even let the cameras film the babies. And Oliva, who had never asked for anything but to live in anonymity like his neighbors, felt the eyes of the entire world riveted on him and his family.

In spite of Dr. Dafoe's somber prognostications, the quints, born two months premature, survived in a house with no running water or electricity. But the Dionnes needed incubators, medical equipment, and nurses to take care of the babies and their mother. They had to send a request to hospitals in Toronto and Montreal for the mother's milk that Elzire wasn't able to produce. And then, they had to clothe and feed the five little girls.

16

Obsessed by all these costs, which he had no way of meeting, Oliva was utterly desperate. He therefore agreed, at the urging of the village priest, who acted as his negotiator, to an offer from an American promoter: he would receive a salary and a percentage of the profits if he exhibited the quints at the Chicago World's Fair when they were strong enough to make the trip. Dr. Dafoe told him to sign: "It'll give you some money right away, and your family needs it. In any case, the babies won't survive."

Oliva repudiated the contract the day after he signed it, since Elzire wanted nothing to do with it. But the newspapers got wind of the affair and created a scandal. They portrayed Oliva as an illiterate peasant — he who had a ninth-grade education! — and a boor who thought nothing of exploiting his children. Dr. Dafoe did not mention that he had advised Oliva. On the contrary, he stated that, as long as he was their doctor, the quintuplets would never take the trip to Chicago.

From that point on, life was hell for Oliva. He felt as though the whole world was against him. On the other hand, Dr. Dafoe became a hero: the humble country physician, selflessly devoted and capable of performing miracles. Dafoe took things in hand, and Oliva soon found himself a stranger in his own home, which was transformed into a hospital. Even poor Elzire was pushed aside: she wasn't allowed to take care of her quints, or even to hold them in her arms. And Dr. Dafoe insisted that the five other children be sent away to live with relatives.

A month later, the Ontario government used the pretext of the "Chicago contract" to take over the guardianship of the quintuplets from their parents for a period of two years. Oliva and Elzire had to appear before a judge, who led them to believe that if they didn't sign the necessary papers, the assistance of the government would be withdrawn. Since it was only for two years, they reluctantly gave in and signed.

A guardianship council was created and the hospital was built across the road: The Dafoe Hospital and Nursery! It was an establishment designed exclusively for the Dionne quintuplets. Behind the chain-link fence and the gate guarded by armed policemen — it was feared that the quintuplets would be kidnapped as the Lindbergh child had been — Dr. Dafoe ruled supreme. For many months, Elzire and Oliva could see their girls only through a bay window, as they learned their first words from their nurses and took their first steps into the nurses' open arms. Elzire was sick with rage. On the other hand, the photographer from the news agency that had obtained an exclusive contract could spend as much time with the quints as he wanted, as could the actors and crew from 20th-Century Fox, who were shooting a feature film on the birth of the Dionne quintuplets, a film in which Dr. Dafoe would be the hero.

As the curious flowed in from across North America, the quints were exhibited on the stoop, held out by the nurses. These visitors made money for the entire region, and the nurses earned a king's ransom in fees and royal-ties. The 20th-Century Fox studios had paid $250,000 to use the babies in five films. A fortune was accumulating in the trust fund set up for the quintuplets.

Perhaps because they attracted almost as many tourists as Niagara Falls, the Ontario government insisted on extending the guardianship of the quintuplets to their eighteenth birthday. The Dionne family was divided, it seemed, forever. On one side of the road, the five little girls lived like princesses, raised by strangers, flooded with gifts, and surrounded by wealth. On the other side of the road, the Dionne family, to which two more children were soon added, led a reclusive, pariah-like existence.

All of this was in the past, but, in spite of his desire to move on, Oliva felt that the past would never be far from his mind, or his heart. What patience it had taken to turn things around, to make public opinion and the government see a Dionne family reunion as desirable! Today, he was, to all intents and purposes, alone at the helm: his girls had been returned to him, and he was managing their $900,000 fortune, which, he felt, should be used to benefit the entire family. Clearly, the government agreed, since it had authorized construction of the new house and the purchase of furniture from the quints' fund. However, there were things that money could not buy, wounds that would never heal.

As Oliva contemplated the house with the peaked roof where he had lived for seven years, he felt like a cornered animal. There had been fewer tourists since the war had brought rationing of gasoline and tires. He was thinking of transforming the old house into a museum to bring them back. Although he had strongly protested the exhibition of his children before millions of visitors, he, too, had profited from the windfall by opening two souvenir shops, where he sold even his own autograph. And he didn't want it to end. He had plans for the "little girls": he wanted to make them stars of stage and screen. To do so, he had to keep their names in the news and manage their appearances carefully. He knew he could do it. He had become an expert in the art of public relations over the last few years.

• • •

The door slammed, and Marie awoke with a start. A second later, the harsh glare of the ceiling light stung her eyes. She rolled over, blinked, and, her heart in her throat, wondered where she was. Then she recognized the room and her sister Lucie, who had just come in.

"Good night," she said, trying to be friendly.

"Exactly. Good night," Lucie answered.

Marie put her head on her pillow, closed her eyes, and tried to go back to sleep. She so much wanted to enter that pleasant refuge. Turning toward the wall, she shut her eyes tight, but the light permeated her eyelids. And then Lucie opened and closed the squeaking drawers of the bureau, noisily moving things around. She left the bathroom door open, its light adding to the brightness in the room. The sound of the tap, the toilet, another door. Simone, whose room was on the other side of the bathroom, joined Lucie, and they loudly discussed the arrival of the "little girls."

"It was fine when it was just us! We should have . . ."

Marie blocked her ears with her hands and silently hummed the "Moonlight Sonata," which the nurses often played in the evening on the hospital phonograph. She thought of the beloved face of Miss Corriveau, whose severity couldn't disguise her warm heart, and of Miss Michaud, with its soft features. The memories of all the women to whom she had been attached and who had, one by one, left her life, flooded into Marie's mind: caressing hands, gentle voices, affectionate words, laughter, songs, games. All these fragments converged into a single memory that no longer had a face but still had a name: Yvonne Leroux. It was more a diffuse yet powerful impression than a memory of perfect happiness. It was a feeling of warmth, a scent, the traces of great love. Also, the pain of abandonment. Yvonne Leroux, who had been there since the day after they were born, had left when they were only two and a half years old; for the quints, it had been like the death of an adored mother. Her face had been erased from Marie's memory, but her love had left an indelible imprint on the girl's heart and flesh. Tonight, she was missed, along with Yvonne, Annette, Émilie, and Cécile. How nice it would be to sleep near the others, or even to try to sleep hearing their breathing in the dark! Pulling her blanket over her head, Marie wept silently.

• • •

Quintland, the "quintuplets' kingdom," comprised some fifteen wooden buildings in the middle of fields surrounded by forest. On venturing out there from Callander, a village about ten miles from North Bay, Ontario, one saw first, on the right, the buildings of the Dionne farm and the house where the quints were born. A little farther on were Oliva's two souvenir shops. On the other side of the road were the nurses' residence, the police sentry box, the U-shaped observation gallery, and finally the store belonging to the two midwives who had assisted Elzire at the birth.

Quintland: a magical name for hundreds of thousands of visitors who, every summer, rushed into the dark hallway of the observation gallery to spend a few minutes contemplating the carefree games of "their" quints. When they left, their eyes moist with emotion, their hearts full, they knew that they were the envy of their friends, who had to content themselves with photographs and films of the miraculous children. Even Hollywood stars came to visit the "Canadian royal family" in their hospital. In the 1930s, with the upheaval of the terrible economic depression and growing instability in Europe, the "miracle of Corbeil" — or "miracle of Callander," for the English — was a hopeful sign. The weekly reports on the quintuplets were often the only good news in the newspapers.

The little girls were a tourist attraction that injected $25 million into the Ontario provincial economy every year. Thanks to them, the North Bay region had found prosperity, while the rest of North America was still suffering the effects of the Depression. And the best part was that, with their income from advertising, photographs, and films, the quintuplets themselves paid for maintenance of the hospital and the salaries of the nine people who looked after them and their interests, including those of the provincial policemen standing guard outside their door!

Things had changed, as the silhouette of the "big house" that now towered over Quintland testified. With the war on people's minds, and perhaps because the quints had lost the charming faces of childhood, they had lost some of their attraction in the eyes of many people, and the flow of tourists had slowed over the last two years. From the government's point of view, returning guardianship of the girls to their father now represented less of an economic loss. Furthermore, converted little by little to the parents' cause by the campaign that Oliva and his allies had waged, public opinion had come to support a Dionne family reunion, something it had judged objectionable just a few short years before.

The next morning, a great calm reigned over Quintland as the Dionne children left for school.

Oliva Dionne could not bring himself to let the quintuplets go to the village school, where they would be in contact with other children, so he had obtained permission from the Department of Education to turn the hospital into a private school reserved exclusively for his twelve children, paid for out of the quints' fund. For teachers, he had hired nuns from Nicolet, Quebec, mistrusting those from North Bay. He mistrusted everyone.

For Armand, the peacefulness of the morning brought to mind the happy times before the quints were born. He had been almost eight years old at the time, and he remembered all the fuss that had followed the event and disrupted his life. With time, the bitterness within had been transformed into a sort of apathy.

The sun, still low on the horizon, made the thick frost that covered the grass sparkle. When they had gone through the gate into the hospital grounds, Serge, Roger, and Laurent began to run off the path, turning circles in the hay made brittle by the frost. Simone and Lucie followed, huddled together and whispering. Then came Annette and Cécile, walking on either side of Marie. Behind them, Yvonne held Émilie's hand. The two eldest, Armand and Rachel, brought up the rear.

Once outside, Émilie felt as though she could breathe again. It was as if she had been gasping for air since arriving in the brick house the previous evening. She couldn't wait to be within the familiar walls of the old hospital and see the friendly faces of the nuns. The hours of classes, which even yesterday she had considered time stolen from her life, now seemed like liberation. She had a feeling that she would have trouble getting used to her new life, although she didn't know why.

Armand's flat voice drifted to them. "Our family was happy before you were born, you quints," he said in English.

Émilie gave Yvonne's hand a squeeze as she gave her sister a look that told her not to get angry.

"That's true!" Rachel added. "After giving birth to you, Mom stayed fat. It tired her out. Five at a time, it's not natural!"

Émilie knew that it wasn't their fault, but she didn't dare say so out loud.

Then Armand sneered, "A litter!" He and Rachel laughed. "You caused lots of problems for the old man," he said. "All those problems have made him old before his time."

"I remember when we went to see you in the nursery," Rachel said. "You ran behind the nurses' skirts when Mom called you over. That's hard for a mother. So many times I saw her come back home bawling like a calf!"

As soon as Rachel stopped, Armand picked up the thought. "For sure, the grief ruined her health, not to mention her character! She has no patience left."

"Without you," Rachel concluded, "things would have been much better."

Not understanding why they were the object of such spiteful talk, Émilie began to sniffle. Yvonne turned toward the older children and shouted, "Okay, that's enough!"

"Oh, I'm *scared*!" said Rachel, laughing.

She had not forgotten the affront she'd suffered when she was ten, though at the time she'd felt only immense disappointment. The entire family had been invited to meet the King and Queen of England. Their mother had

24

bought suits for the boys and made long dresses for the girls. They had taken a special train. There was a special luxury car for the quints, and in Toronto, they'd led the parade in a convertible automobile — after all, they were the ones for whom the crowds lined the streets, cheering and waving flags. The others were used to this. But once they were inside the provincial parliament buildings, an official in a gold-braided coat told Elzire that only the quints, their parents, their nurses, and Dr. Dafoe could meet the royals; the other children would not be admitted. Rachel and the others had been dreaming of this moment for weeks. That was when she began to hate her sisters. Everything was always for them!

The younger boys calmed down as they neared the old nurses' residence, which had been transformed into a home for the nuns who were their teachers.

On the schoolhouse steps, Sister Aimée-des-Anges was vigorously ringing the bell. Armand came running, followed by the others. Only Yvonne remained behind, wiping Émilie's eyes with her handkerchief, along with Rachel, who was watching them and savoring the effect of her attacks.

Before going in, Rachel made one last jab. "You should have stayed where you were. We didn't need you."

Once she was alone with her sister, Yvonne told her, "Don't pay any attention to what they say, Émilie."

"But it hurts."

"Make believe it doesn't. The more we react, the more they'll do it. Soon they'll get tired."

"You think so?"

"Come on, we'll be late," said Yvonne, not knowing how to answer.

• • •

The days rolled on: one week passed, then a second. With their daily trips between home and the hospital, the children beat a narrow path through the snow. Annette felt as though she were a train that always traveled along the same track. For the first time in her life, she felt like a prisoner. When she thought of the future, she saw only an endless repetition of the same motions.

Going through the gates brought no sense of freedom; it was as though the whole world were one vast prison. The quints knew nothing about the real world, having left their hospital only three times: once, when they were five years old for a trip to Toronto; then two years later, again to Toronto, to stimulate sales of Victory Bonds; and this year, they had gone to Superior, Wisconsin, to launch five ships bearing their names that were bound for England. In front of a crowd of fifteen thousand, they had suddenly become aware that they were objects of curiosity, and rather than feeling flattered, they felt self-conscious.

Since moving to the "big house," the quints had been going with their family to Sunday mass in Corbeil. But what pleasure could they take in this outing, when a police car always preceded their father's Cadillac? When policemen stood guard behind the nave during the service? Anything to draw attention! Perhaps it flattered their father, made him feel important. But the quints would have preferred to go unnoticed, not to be stared at all the time. They kept their eyes riveted to their missals, which kept their mother from nagging, in a low voice, "Don't turn around! Look straight ahead!"

Like her sisters, Annette couldn't get used to the glacial atmosphere in the house, to the quarrels that broke out constantly among the other members of the family, to the hard, hurtful language that they used with each other. And very often, the quints, who played no part in these squabbles, ended up being blamed. They began to believe that everything that was wrong in the family was their fault, just as their brothers and sisters claimed.

On top of that, they were teased about their taste in music and food, which differed from the rest of the household's. The other children spoke English perfectly, as their father used it with them, and they poked fun at the quintuplets, who were not comfortable with the language, since Oliva had forbidden it to be taught to them in the hospital. Oliva was well aware that Dr. Dafoe spoke only English, and perhaps that was part of his decision. When they were six, on orders from Elzire, they had refused to greet the mothers of North America in English during a live Mother's Day radio broadcast. On the air, Yvonne carefully pronounced, in English, the reason for their refusal: "It's not nice to speak English."

Although it was never said out loud, Marie, Émilie, Cécile, Yvonne, and Annette knew very well what their mother and father expected from them: they should show affection and love, they should be happy to be back in the bosom of their family. But their parents did nothing to inspire such feelings; they merely went through the motions. Nevertheless, the quints' respect was real and sincere, and their obedience was a way of expressing it.

Their parents kept the five girls from being alone together, insisting over and over that they were no dif- ferent from their brothers and sisters. However, they continued to call them "the little girls" and to dress them and style their hair identically. While the others did their homework in their rooms, the quints had to sit at the dining-room table, under their mother's watchful eye, distracted by the radio, to which their father was always listening. As well, their sisters and brothers could leave the house half an hour before school began to talk to the nuns, but the quints had to stay home until the bell had sounded. A thousand little details made it clear that their parents were lying when they claimed to treat them just like the others.

• • •

One Friday afternoon at the beginning of December, Mr. Sasse arrived from New York to photograph the quintuplets in the bosom of their family. He had been making the trip to Quintland several times a year since his agency had obtained exclusive photography rights almost four years earlier. Before that, when the newspapers and magazines couldn't get enough pictures of the quintuplets, a competing agency had kept a photographer permanently on site. Now that there was less demand, Mr. Sasse came only to mark the important events in the girls' lives: their birthday, Christmas, Easter, Thanksgiving. With the much-anticipated reunion of the Dionne family, Sasse had an angle, and he intended to exploit it to the fullest.

Warned in advance of his visit, Elzire and Oliva welcomed Sasse like an honored guest, almost a friend. Without taking sides openly, he had always shown sympathy for their cause and had been rather distant with Dr. Dafoe. No doubt, he could see that the doctor's reign in the hospital was drawing to a close. One of the few outsiders whom Oliva didn't mistrust, Sasse had been the first to photograph the parents with their quintuplets (something that the contracts signed with the guardianship council, and by Oliva with different agencies, had not permitted). And Elzire felt that he had always taken flattering pictures of her.

"The roads weren't too bad?" she asked him, wiping her hands on her apron.

"I didn't even notice, I was so looking forward to eating your food again."

"You're exaggerating," she protested, clearly pleased.

"Not at all. But I'm afraid I might have to inconvenience you over the next couple of days, Mrs. Dionne. We'll have to change their hair and clothes a few times. To get a little variety."

"No problem, Mr. Sasse. It will be my pleasure."

"Are you taking pictures of the whole family?" asked Oliva. It was more a statement than a question.

"Of course! I want images that reflect the joy of the reunion, the happiness of the quints, the happy family, a peaceful daily life. Maybe you, Mrs. Dionne, teaching them to cook. The whole family around the table. Things like that."

This answer thrilled Oliva, since it was the impression of a united family that he wanted to give, even though it wasn't yet reality. It would come, though; he knew it. He picked up the visitor's suitcase.

"I'll show you to your room. The little girls are still in school. If you want to rest a little before dinner . . ."

"It's not necessary, but thank you. I'd like you to show me the house, so I have an idea of the layout. Then I can choose my angles."

"For dinner, we're having the moose Oliva killed this autumn," Elzire told him as she headed for the kitchen.

The photographer followed Oliva upstairs, glancing into the living room as he passed.

"It's a magnificent house, Mr. Dionne. The public will

29

love the life that you've created for the quints."

A shrewd observer, the photographer noticed the great sadness in the eyes of the quintuplets when they thought no one was watching them. Their faces, which had been so open and calm at the hospital, were marked by melancholy, and their attitude and bearing revealed a sort of resignation. But they were truly professional models: as soon as the camera was focused on them, they instinctively adopted the poses that fit the scene. Sitting around their father, who was presenting them with a dog, they looked delighted and interested. When they simulated a sewing lesson with their mother, Sasse didn't need to tell them how to act: they seemed concentrated on their work — even though they had never before held needle and thread. And sitting on the carpet in the big living room, each held her Shirley Temple doll in her arms and smiled the brilliant smile of a satisfied child, eyes sparkling.

The photography sessions lasted two days! Annette had had enough of these shams, but she knew that if the photographer was happy, her parents would be happy, too. Doing what was expected of her meant avoiding criticism and scolding. What she found hardest was seeing, out of the corner of her eye, a brother or sister out of Mr. Sasse's sight, giving the quints a look of envy or scorn. And she was irritated by her mother's rough gestures as she braided the girls' hair, then undid the braids to curl it with an iron.

Finally, the sessions were over. Mr. Sasse left, and the quints were getting ready to go to their rooms, when their father gestured for them to stop. *He'll praise us for our patience,* Annette told herself, waiting for the first compliment he would ever give them. Instead, he said, in his usual emotionless voice, "Dr. Dafoe is dead."

Annette was shocked, and she could tell that her sisters were, too. Other feelings fought to show on their faces, and their father seemed to be waiting for them to betray their emotions so that he could get angry. Annette hurried to distract him.

"When did it happen, Dad?" she asked in a noncommittal tone.

"In June."

Six months ago! And they had been told nothing. Annette kept her face impassive, as if the news had had no effect on her. Her sisters did the same. Satisfied, because he didn't want them to be attached to anyone outside the family — especially his old enemy — Oliva Dionne walked away.

The girls went up to their rooms in silence. But once they were out of sight of the others, they exchanged woebegone looks. There was no question of saying anything: the walls had ears in this house, and anything you said would come back to haunt you sooner or later.

Marie went to her room and made sure that Lucie wasn't in the bathroom. Then she knelt beside her bed, put her face in her cupped hands, and let the tears flow. She tried to pray, but images crowded into her mind. She saw the doctor, who, as far back as she could remember, had come to see them twice a day. His old hat was too small for his big head, his suit was always rumpled, and he smelled of tobacco smoke. His pipe was always clamped between his lips, under his gray mustache. He laughed and talked softly. Yvonne had always said that Marie was the favorite of the man they called first "Da-da" and then, once they had learned to speak more clearly, "Dotteur." Was she his favorite? It didn't matter whether it was true or not, she had loved him dearly — even if, in recent years, she couldn't show it because it displeased Mom and Dad, and even if his visits to the hospital had become less frequent. Marie finally remembered the words to the "Our Father" and she recited the prayer.

• • •

In the neighboring room, Émilie and Yvonne talked softly, their voices trembling a little.

"He wasn't old, was he, Yvonne?"

"At least sixty. He'd been quite sick lately."

Émilie nodded her head distractedly. She was thinking of the doctor's last visit, more than a year and a half ago. It had been February or March. There had been snow on the ground, and construction of the "big house" had just begun. She had bitter memories, and some guilty feelings, about that meeting.

"It's not our fault," Yvonne murmured, guessing what her sister was thinking.

Miss Vézina had remained standing in the doorway, and the implication had been clear for Émilie. Their teacher, a friend of their parents, was observing the meeting; she would report everything to their mother and father. It would be better to act cold and distant, even if they didn't want to, even if it obviously bothered their old friend.

"He must have understood," Yvonne added, finishing aloud her sister's thought.

"I hope so," said Émilie, on the verge of tears.

"If he didn't know then, he knows now."

It was true. Émilie hadn't thought of it, but now, Dr. Dafoe was watching them from Heaven. He saw that she was crying. He knew how much they had suffered from the conflict among their parents, him, and the

32

nurses. If he had loved them, as she believed, he had forgiven them for their feigned indifference. And even if he was a Protestant, it would make him happy to see that they were praying for him.

"We should recite a rosary," suggested Émilie, reaching to the bureau for her crystal rosary beads.

"You're right."

• • •

The light was already out in Cécile and Annette's room.

"Are you sleeping?" Annette whispered.

No response. She envied her sister, who had managed to take refuge in sleep. Unless she was making believe. Annette tried not to think about Dr. Dafoe: she wanted to remember him bit by bit over the next few days, so that it wouldn't hurt so much. He was dead, *departed* — the word spun around in her head like an electric train on a circular track. It was an image that applied so well to their life — moving and yet standing still! Before, they had always stayed in one spot, and the world had come to them. Come, and then left again, giving the impression of constant change. But no longer.

It seemed to Annette that her life, which she couldn't separate from the lives of her sisters, was just a series of departures. Departures of others, not them. A series of abandonments. All those who seemed to love them ended up disappearing from their world. Others replaced them, but each time, it became more difficult, more costly, to become attached to them. Only Dr. Dafoe had stayed loyal. Now he, too, after appearing more and more rarely, had left. His final departure marked, better than anything else, the end of their old life.

She repeated, a little louder, "Are you sleeping, Cécile?"

2

"It's Mary's month, the most beautiful month . . ." Émilie
hummed as she dipped her hand in the bathwater to
check the temperature. This hymn had been running
through her head since the prayer ceremony at the foot
of the Virgin, housed in an artificial grotto behind the
house. The nuns led these devotional exercises every
evening in the month of May, and the entire Dionne
family attended.

"This time, someone else should go first," said Émilie
insistently, turning toward Annette, Cécile, and Yvonne,
who were looking at her gravely.

"Not a chance!" retorted Yvonne. "You first."

Her two sisters nodded in agreement. Their mother had
ordered all four of them to take their bath in the same
water. Since it got cold quickly, the last one in was
treated to a quick, frigid dip. Because she was the most
delicate and ill the most often, the others had decided
that Émilie would always go first. Marie took her bath
after Lucie, who seemed to tarry, deliberately, until the

water was less than lukewarm and gray with dissolved soap.

"Anyway —" said Annette, in a tone that the others knew only too well.

Cécile quickly interrupted. "Imagine how much coal it would take to heat up water for fourteen baths," she said in a conciliatory tone. "There are already nineteen rooms to heat."

"But we're the only ones who don't get clean water!" protested Annette. "The others . . ." She let her words trail off and cocked an ear toward the hallway.

Yvonne took advantage of her silence to say, in a low voice, "That's the way it is. We'll just have to cope with it."

"I wonder if Dad knows about this," Annette said pointedly.

Yvonne frowned darkly at her sister. "Don't ever tell him!" she warned.

"Don't make things worse, Annette," Cécile added. Then she abandoned her concerned look and changed the subject. "A pony!" She smiled.

"Oh, yes . . ." Annette sighed dreamily, imagining herself galloping through the fields beyond the fences topped with barbed wire: sometimes she was a cowgirl, sometimes a princess wearing a fairy-tale hat and veil. They all smiled, enchanted by the prospect of having an animal of their very own. The household's two dogs, Carlo, a St. Bernard, and Bichonne, a Great Dane, were guard dogs that lived outside.

"The newspapers say it's a female," Cécile said. "What'll we call her?"

The four girls looked questioningly at each other and mutely decided that Marie would get to name it, so she wouldn't feel excluded from the group.

They had read about the gift that they would receive for their tenth birthday, the following week, in the North Bay newspaper, the *Nugget*, the publisher of which was a friend of their father's. It was also in the pages of the *Nugget* that they had found out what their New Year's gifts would be. They sometimes found in the newspaper what they were supposed to have said and felt about finally being in the bosom of their family. Other times, they read news about themselves that they were the last to know.

"Émilie!" Yvonne called from their room. "Where did you hide my Shirley Temple? It's not funny!"

"I didn't touch it."

Émilie rushed to their room, the other two on her heels, and saw that her own doll was no longer on her bed. She looked in the cupboard. Not there. Annette went to her room and quickly returned, looking dumfounded.

"Mine's gone, too! And so's Cécile's!"

"Who did this?" Cécile exclaimed angrily.

Silence. The answer seemed obvious. They all looked at Yvonne, who realized that they were counting on her. Taking a deep breath, she went to the door. Marie came out of her room when she heard her sister's footsteps in the hall. From her upset expression, Yvonne knew what had happened. She gave Marie a reassuring pat.

"Ours, too. I'll take care of it."

She knocked on the door of her parents' large bedroom. No response. They were downstairs. With every step she descended, Yvonne felt her determination melting away.

Elzire was sitting at the dining-room table doing the bookkeeping for the quintuplets' trust fund, which her husband managed. The end of the month was approaching, and the auditor appointed by the government, Percy

Wilson, would be coming to check the books. It was just a formality; nothing to worry about. Wilson was very accommodating. "He's the answer to our prayers," Oliva would say.

"Mom?"

"Now what?" Elzire asked brusquely, without lifting her eyes from her papers.

Self-conscious, Yvonne could dredge up only a thin thread of a voice to say, "Our Shirley Temples . . ."

"Gone!"

"Why?" Gripped by a wave of emotion, Yvonne could not help raising her voice.

Elzire turned and gave her a piercing look. Scared that her mother might explode, as so often happened, Yvonne instinctively took a step backward. But the loss she had suffered was too great for her to hold her tongue.

"We've had them for years, we love them," she pleaded. "They're the only thing we have."

"The only thing you have!" Elzire laughed. "You've always had everything! They've spoiled you rotten. If I'd raised you, you'd be normal, like the others."

Yvonne had an image of herself as a little girl in the hospital playground. She could hear Elzire talking to Annette, who had just hurt herself. Her mother refused to console her: "I don't love you as a daughter." It was hard for her to hold back her tears.

"Our dolls . . ." she pleaded.

Elzire wouldn't budge.

"You are no longer children. Those dolls are not for girls of your age. Me, when I was ten, I was doing the work of a man in the fields, and on top of that the work of a woman in the house. Don't complain!"

Yvonne gave up, but she didn't move. Elzire slapped

37

the palm of her hand on the varnished wood table and ordered, dryly, "Go to your room!"

The girl jumped, turned on her heel, and left, her head hanging. She knew that nothing would change her mother's mind. Still, she could consider herself lucky; things might have turned out worse. Elzire had a quick temper and a heavy hand . . .

When they saw Yvonne's face, the others knew right away what it meant. Cécile gave her a hug, and Yvonne, the strong one, the decisive one, sobbed on her shoulder. All of them loved their dolls, but no one was more attached to hers than Yvonne. They had been five years old when they'd got them, and she had been fascinated to discover that a person could be reproduced many times and yet remain unique; the dolls in their own images always came in sets of five. With her Shirley Temple, Yvonne created a one-to-one intimacy that broke the tight circle of the five sisters. When she was frustrated, she consoled herself by comforting her doll; the tenderness and affection that were sometimes lacking in her life could be obtained by giving them to her Shirley.

"The water will be cold," Cécile said to Émilie, who disappeared into the bathroom.

Cécile gave Annette a look that said to leave. Annette was happy to go. Witnessing her sister's unhappiness was too painful; she had enough of her own.

Cécile gently patted Yvonne's back. Yvonne muttered, between hiccups, "What do I have left?"

"You have us," Cécile answered, holding her tighter.

• • •

To mark the tenth birthday of the quintuplets to whom science hadn't given two days to live, newspapers and

38

magazines from all over North America published photographs and articles. Once again, the vicissitudes of their
birth were recounted, the major events of their early years
were related, a story a thousand times told, embellished or
distorted to the point that even they who were the main
actors were no longer certain of their own memories.

In Quintland — or Dionneville, as the French papers
called it in order to show their support for the parents —
the birthday party was simple. Besides the family, there
were only a few guests: Lilian Barker, a reporter from
New York who had been an ally of Elzire and Oliva's
since 1934 and had written a book taking their side;
Mr. Sasse, with his camera; and Father Gustave Sauvé,
who had come all the way from Ottawa without even
waiting for an invitation.

An influential member of the French-Canadian Educa-
tional Association of Ontario who had supported Oliva
and Elzire's cause since 1937, the priest was at home
at the Dionnes'. At the height of the battle between
Dr. Dafoe and Oliva, he had visited the quints in the hospital. He had been mandated by his association to advise
the parents and make sure that the children were being
raised in the Catholic faith and speaking French. Since
then, he had come several times a year to be a discreet
observer. His visits had become a normal part of life, and,
although he had no specific status, no one questioned his
presence in Corbeil.

Oliva mistrusted him, as he did all strangers, particularly priests and nuns who might have any influence on
"his" quints. But how could he keep Father Sauvé away
from them without seeming ungrateful? The priest was
very careful never to question Oliva's authority or give
him reason for alarm. And all the children liked his

visits, since he brought films to show them: westerns to please the boys, musical comedies for the girls.

On this day, after the movie was shown in the basement playroom, Annette stayed behind when her brothers and sisters left. The priest began to rewind the reels of the film. Bald, with a fringe of fine hair, Father Sauvé had a broad face that gave an impression of kindness and serenity. Annette watched him as he manipulated the projector with precise movements. Although she had known him as long as she could remember, he still intimidated her; when he talked to her, it seemed that he could see right through her. And although his voice was calm and composed, it exuded authority.

Aware of the little girl's presence, the priest waited a long moment before letting on. Since she was silent, he said, seemingly absorbed in his work, "Did you like the film, Annette?"

"Yes, Father Sauvé."

He waited until he had the projector's motor running, but she still didn't say anything. When the machine was humming, Annette glanced over at the stairs. She was no longer so sure about her decision to tell him that she and her sisters weren't happy living with their family, that they weren't nice to them, and that they would like to go back to the hospital, or to a boarding school.

"Did you want to talk to me, little Annette?"

"Uh . . ." she mumbled, surprised.

"You know, even when we aren't in confession, anything you say to a priest is a secret."

But she didn't want him to keep it a secret, she wanted him to act. And suddenly, the possible consequences occurred to her: yelling, blame, tears, spanking. And what if the priest couldn't change anything? Her father was so

40

powerful that everyone was scared of him.

"I am your friend," the priest insisted gently. "You can talk to me."

Annette heard the heavy footsteps of her mother making the parquet of the living-room floor above their heads squeak.

"I wanted to tell you . . . I'm glad you came to our birthday party." She made her escape, skipping out of the room. "I think they're calling me."

The priest watched her leave, perplexed.

● ● ●

When they were taken outside to be given their birthday present, the quints pretended to be surprised when they saw their pony, but their joy was real. With her long mane and her tail almost touching the ground, she was even more beautiful than they had imagined her. Marie wanted to call her Belle, and the others immediately agreed. After patting her, all five ran to give their father and mother a kiss, thanking them again and again. Armand, the eldest, held the bridle while Oliva lifted each of the girls into the saddle in turn. Mr. Sasse's camera clicked continuously, capturing the beaming faces.

The quints soon had to tear themselves away from this pleasure to cut the birthday cake their mother had made. As they ate, they cast frequent glances out the window at their pony, which was grazing on the grass at the edge of the driveway. Time seemed to stand still. And then there were guests to be seen out to their cars, to wave at as they pulled away.

Free at last! The quints ran over to Belle.

"Have to put her in the stable," Oliva declared, gesturing for Armand to see to this.

"But Dad, we just got her," the little girls protested in unison.

"She has to rest."

"Can't we take her back with Armand?"

"We'll brush her," added Marie, quivering with impatience.

"No!"

That "no" cracked like a whip. The quints dropped their eyes. No one in the house answered back or stood up to Dad.

"It's not your pony," Oliva said.

Their hearts skipped a beat; had they misheard him?

"What do you mean, Dad?" Cécile asked in a polite little voice.

"I bought it for Roger."

Roger jumped for joy, while Laurent ran inside, bitterly disappointed. His father thought of him as the black sheep of the family, he told the others; this was just more proof.

"A horse isn't for girls!" Roger exclaimed triumphantly to the quints.

Frozen to the spot, they watched their young brother climb onto "their" pony as Armand led it by the bridle to the barn behind the old, deserted house on the other side of the road. Although they had barely touched Belle, they felt as though their hearts were breaking. How could he do this to them?

"Here's your present," their father announced.

He pointed to Simone and Lucie, who were turning the corner of the house pushing bicycles.

"Two bicycles: the five of you will have to make do with them. I don't want to hear any complaints."

"We couldn't afford to buy five," Elzire explained, seeing the girls' disappointment.

Forcing themselves to smile, the quints thanked their parents again, this time for the bicycles.

"It's my pleasure," replied Oliva. But they were forbidden to leave the yard with them, or else . . .

The idea of bicycling on the road hadn't even occurred to them. They weren't even allowed to go through the gate, which was always closed with a huge padlock!

As Annette sat on one bicycle and Cécile and Yvonne held it balanced, the pony neighed. *She's saying goodbye,* Annette thought, her heart full of such mutiny that she felt guilty. They knew that they had nothing of their own; everything could be taken away from them at any time. As a result, they should not get attached to anything.

• • •

Every second Sunday, Grandpa Legros, Elzire's father, came for dinner. After mass, a quarrel always broke out between Elzire and Oliva, who didn't like his father-in-law and found a thousand terrible things to say about him. And every Sunday, once dinner was over, Oliva got into his Cadillac and drove off, without telling anyone where he was going. Elzire never asked him, and perhaps she didn't want to know — or else she already knew. He was never back by the time the quints went to bed. Since it was Armand's day off from looking after the farm, Elzire and the other children had to feed the animals and milk the cows.

When Oliva was away, their mother was less tense, sometimes even forgetting herself to the point of laughing. It was almost as if, like the rest of the family, she was afraid of her husband. The strange thing was that he seemed to be afraid of her, too. They acted a little like accomplices to a crime who didn't trust each other. Since the Dionne reunion, six months ago, Oliva had been more and more frustrated. Morose and taciturn, he smiled only in the presence of strangers and for the cameras.

The conflict that the quints had always sensed between their parents worsened, and they felt responsible. Everything in Elzire and Oliva's attitudes confirmed this feeling. During their frequent fights, the "little girls" always ended up being mentioned, no matter what the subject of the quarrel. The quints vaguely perceived some sort of guilt in their parents, as if they thought they had sinned by bringing them into the world. Over time, the girls developed a sense of shame at having been born five at a time. Each secretly dreamed of being an only child. On the other hand, they could not imagine things otherwise, since they had no idea what real family life was. Even living with the nine other Dionnes around them, they felt like orphans.

Like their father's hopes, their own had been disappointed. Never would they be accepted as full members of the family, treated on an equal footing with the others. On the contrary, everything was done to make them feel inferior. They no longer expected signs of tenderness and affection from their parents. They knew that they would never come to feel total love for them — respect, perhaps, but fear would always be there, too.

Taking the key that always hung from a nail on the wall of the kitchen, Elzire opened the lock that closed the gate. "Aren't all these colors pretty?" she said, pointing at the profusion of wildflowers on either side of the road.

A dreamy smile came over her face as she stepped aside to let her children out. Except for Armand, who was probably loafing around in the village, and Simone and Lucie, who couldn't be found, they were all there.

The boys went first, running across the road and rough-housing.

"Stop your fighting!" Rachel shouted, echoing her mother.

The quints stayed close behind Elzire.

Sunday was finally coming to an end, Cécile noted with relief. There had been no great dramas today. Saturdays and Sundays always made her a little nervous. Being at home wasn't like school, where the nuns made rules and stuck to them and the girls always knew what to expect. In the house, everything was arbitrary: something that was the rule one day might fly out the window the next. It was difficult to know how to act; you never knew what was in store for you.

Cécile was exhausted from fending off trouble for her sisters and herself, trying to smooth out difficulties, defuse potential conflicts, and anticipate her parents' wishes — greasing the wheels in order to avoid as many reprimands and recriminations as possible.

Sunday evenings seemed like an oasis to her: Monday, and school, were just around the corner. And on Sundays they did chores in the barn with their mother, which was a great treat. Aside from trips in their father's car, this was their only opportunity to set foot outside the compound. What a pleasure to hear the gate squeak, to see it open before them, and then to feel underfoot the gravel road that stretched to the horizon in both directions, leading to who knew where . . . For a too-brief instant, they had a sense of lightness — perhaps a taste of freedom.

"I'd like some berries," said Elzire, a little out of breath. "Soon it'll be time for the strawberries, then the raspberries and blueberries."

"Could we go with you, Mom?"

Elzire turned to Cécile, who had asked, and exclaimed, playfully, "I'm counting on it! Five more pickers!" Then she stopped and gave Marie an icy look. "Not you. It's not worth it to take you. With your cross-eyes, you won't see the strawberries. You'll step on them."

And she began to walk again. Even during her brief good moods, Elzire could not keep herself from saying hurtful things. Marie hung her head. Automatically, Yvonne fell into step beside her sister and took her hand.

The group passed in front of the old, deserted house, which had a sinister look. The verandah, rebuilt several years previously but never painted, had turned the same gray as the clapboard walls, and the wood had been cracked by storms and sun.

The miracle of Corbeil, Cécile thought, looking at the windows, which were as empty as the eye sockets in a cow skull on a heap of stones. She and her sisters, their birth — that was the "miracle." And then there had been the miracle of Émilie's inexplicable and complete recovery from polio when she was five. That miracle was attributable to St. Anne — at least, that was what their mother had said. She had told them that their very existence was a miracle! Cécile often thought that what they needed was another miracle. Day after day, she ruminated on a question to which she could never find an answer, perhaps because it didn't exist: *How can I get my sisters out of here?*

As they approached the garden, Cécile put these vexing thoughts out of her mind. Soon they were all busy weeding and harrowing the vegetable patch. It was one of those rare times when their mother didn't complain about the quality of their work.

Once the garden was weeded to her satisfaction, Elzire

took everyone home. As they walked back by the house where she had lived since she got married, when she was sixteen, and where she had given birth to all of her children, she could not repress a shiver. Recent years had left her with a bitter taste in her mouth.

Perhaps because of the sun sliding toward the horizon, she thought of that May evening ten years ago. Her pregnancy had been going badly, and Dr. Dafoe had ordered her to stay in bed. But the Dionnes didn't have the money to hire help, so she had to keep taking care of her five children, her husband, and the house. That day was a Sunday, and Oliva was away. When she felt the first pains, around midnight, she didn't realize right away what was happening — after all, she wasn't due until July — but it quickly became obvious.

When Oliva came home, a little after two in the morning, she sent him to get her Aunt Donalda, who quickly asked him to fetch Mrs. Lebel, the best midwife in the region. From the distressed expressions of the two women who were so used to bringing children into the world, Elzire knew that things were going badly. The labor pains were not at all like those she had known in her previous six births. She was weakening, losing consciousness for seconds at a time, and she felt herself slipping away. The finality of death and the fear of leaving her children orphaned took over. And she couldn't get her mind off Léo, her fourth child, who had died of pneumonia when he was just one month old.

She wasn't really aware of the birth. When her aunt told her that she had just given birth to five girls, quintuplets, her first thought was, *How will we feed and clothe ten children in this terrible depression?* But when Oliva showed up at her bedside a little later, she had new concerns. "What will people think when they hear about this?" she asked him. "They'll think we're pigs."

Now Elzire looked around her at the countryside, which had been transformed by the birth of the quints. There were souvenir shops, a parking lot, public toilets, the midwives' store, the observation gallery, and the hospital where there had once been pastureland. And now there was the new brick house. These buildings brought back memories of painful, miserable years. Of course, she and Oliva no longer had financial problems, but there were lots of problems of a different kind to take their place!

It was with a bit of nostalgia that she gave the old house another glance. Times gone by . . . They'd been happy and hadn't known it. They'd had their farm, a life with family and friends, they hadn't cared a fig about the world and its newspapers. The days had flowed by peacefully. The door of the house didn't even have a lock. And then, the hordes of strangers! The reporters, the curious, the profiteers, doctors, ministers, lawyers had all invaded the place, taken over, stripped the quints' parents of their God-given rights, divided the family.

Elzire sighed heavily and crossed the road. Again, she had to open the big padlock. Padlocks, gates, fences: she would never get used to the feeling of being a prisoner in her own home.

Even though Oliva wasn't pleased, Elzire was glad that the incessant stream of the curious had dried up. Only a few hundred tourists still made the pilgrimage to Quintland, as one would visit the ruins of an ancient monument. They dropped in at Oliva's souvenir shops and Mrs. Legros's store, photographed the hospital and the observation gallery, then stood in front of the gate to the big house without a hope of seeing or speaking to the quints.

The quints had been trained to go into the house or hide in back when cars drove up. There was no need to force them; they hated the curiosity they aroused. At least, that's what they said. But it must bother them, Elzire told herself, that they were no longer celebrities who visited other celebrities, the focus of all eyes, the object of all attention. She couldn't think of any other reason for the sadness that they never managed to hide completely. Perhaps they felt deserted, abandoned by those who had claimed to love them. But it would pass. They would learn that they were children like the others, and that only their own parents could really and truly love them.

"It's time to milk the cows!" Elzire called to the boys, who ran to the kitchen door.

They stopped to wait for the others, then the group went around the big brick house to the outbuildings behind the new family home.

Cécile loved the barn. Barn work wasn't as awful as housework, and she could almost make a game of it. And the barn cats were always ready to be patted. She wondered, in fact, why they weren't kept in the house.

"I'll go get the cows," Laurent offered.

"No, you muck out. Roger, you bring in the cows."

The boy fumed because once again his brother had been given the pleasant task. To Laurent fell the job of loading manure into a wheelbarrow and dumping it on the pile behind the building.

Cécile found no consolation in the fact that the injustices in the household were not reserved exclusively for her and her sisters. On the contrary, she felt sorry for her brother; she knew exactly how he must feel. It would take so little for harmony and peace to reign in the family — but it was just an idle dream.

While Rachel and Annette helped their mother wash the milk pails and fill the troughs, Émilie, Marie, and Serge fed grain to the chickens and turkeys and corn cobs to the pigs. With pitchforks, Yvonne and Cécile brought straw from the barn and spread it in the stalls for bedding. Then they climbed into the hayloft and played happily in the sweet-smelling hay. Their chore was to throw down the hay near the door to the stable. But, away from their mother's watchful eyes and ears, they enlivened their work with games, jokes, and laughter, recalling their carefree times in the hospital, under the care of the nurses and Dr. Dafoe.

Before climbing down the ladder, Cécile turned to her sister and said, in a serious voice, "I'd like us to be happy. Everyone could be happy."

"That depends on neither you nor me," Yvonne decreed bitterly.

"It seems to me that we're not asking so much."

"And who will you ask, my poor Cécile?"

"If only things were peaceful, it would be one huge step in the right direction."

"You know what I think? All the shouting and arguing, they've always been like that. It's not because we're in the house."

Cécile climbed down the ladder, reflecting on her sister's words. When Yvonne joined her, she said again, her voice low since they were near the door, "The best thing would be to go to boarding school."

"I think about it sometimes," Yvonne answered. "Each of us in a different school."

"Separated?"

"Yes, or else we'll keep on being 'the quints.' Not girls like other girls."

Cécile didn't want to pursue this line of thought. She took a forkful of hay into the barn. Her sister was right, but the prospect of separation made her queasy.

The cows in the stalls mooed when they smelled the hay. Elzire, Rachel, and Annette were milking them. Annette had become so skillful that she no longer had to concentrate on her task. She began to sing: "*Frère Jacques, frère Jacques . . .*"

Before Cécile and Yvonne could take up the round, their mother spoke up. "Stop that, Annette. You'll upset the cows."

This wasn't teasing, it was an order. Yvonne and Cécile looked at each other, puzzled. Why weren't they allowed to sing? Whenever they started to sing as they dried the dishes that their mother was washing, she reacted the same way. According to Sister Saint-Louis, they had pretty voices and sang well. Didn't Elzire like singing?

● ● ●

When her husband wasn't home, Elzire cooked little or not at all. That evening, she served the children the cold ham left over from lunch. And since there were few dishes to wash, she kept only Marie and Émilie to wash them. As the others went up to their rooms, Elzire called after them, "Find Lucie and send her to me. I have something to say to her."

Her tone of voice did not bode well. On the stairs, Annette whispered to Yvonne and Cécile, "For once, it's not us she's mad at . . ."

Warned by Yvonne, Lucie grumbled as she went downstairs. Yvonne followed her at a distance, then stopped halfway down the stairs, where she could hear without being seen. She didn't know why she was doing this, since curiosity was not in her nature.

The voices coming from the kitchen were indistinct at first, then they got louder and the words became intelligible. Lucie was protesting, "It's not my job!"

"Liar!" Elzire shouted. "Don't take me for a fool."

There was a commotion, then Lucie yelled, in a threatening voice, "Touch me just once, you old cow, and Dad will hear about it."

A sudden silence. After a few seconds, Lucie stomped out of the kitchen, muttering, "The damn cow!" She passed Yvonne, who was going downstairs looking as innocent as possible and keeping her eyes off her older sister.

When she got to the foot of the stairs, Yvonne heard her mother shouting angrily, "You never do what I say. I'll teach you!"

Dull noises, protests, crying. Yvonne ran into the kitchen. Her face purple, Elzire was hitting Marie and Émilie, who were retreating and trying to protect their faces with their hands.

"Mom!" Yvonne shouted at the top of her lungs. "What are you doing?"

Elzire froze, her hand in midair. Then, recognizing Yvonne's voice, she turned back to the little girls, who had dropped their defenses. She grabbed Émilie by the arm and hit her hard.

"You little brat, we'll have you locked up in a reform school!"

Without thinking, Yvonne shoved her mother, trying to make her let go and be reasonable.

"Mom! Mom! Stop!"

But Elzire wasn't listening. Stocky and impressively strong, she was not put off by Yvonne's efforts to interpose herself between her and Émilie, at whom she continued to hurl abuse. Yvonne raised her voice above her mother's.

"Mom! Why are you doing this, Mom? Leave her alone!"

Elzire pushed Émilie away and wheeled around toward Yvonne. The others saw their chance to get away.

Without warning, Elzire slapped Yvonne's cheek hard. Yvonne staggered. Her face contorted, Elzire cast a disgusted look at her daughter.

"I'm in charge here! Don't think you can stand up to me because you're your father's favorite!"

A blow from the back of Elzire's hand sent Yvonne to the floor, where she remained for several minutes, semiconscious.

"Why?" she implored as she painfully got to her feet.

Elzire turned her back and started to wash the dishes again.

"Come dry in your sisters' place."

Her cheeks on fire, Yvonne stood as far away as possible from her mother. Although Elzire seemed calm as she stared out the window at the fields that stretched to the edge of the forest, another fit of anger might overtake her at any moment.

Mother and daughter exchanged not a word. Yvonne was obsessed by her unanswered question: Why? Why such rage in Elzire, such relentless rage against the quints? They had done nothing to deserve such punishment. On the contrary, they did their best to please their parents; they did more than their share of household tasks, and they never complained. It seemed that the more goodwill they showed and the more they endured in silence, the more was required of them and the more they were abused.

Should she threaten to complain to their father, as all the others did? Elzire knew that she wouldn't dare, nor would Cécile, Annette, Émilie, or Marie. As well, Yvonne strongly doubted that speaking to their father would change anything. Elzire and he rivaled each other in harshness toward the quints. And if they took this useless step, their mother would take revenge and life would be hell. There was no solution. They had to suffer in silence.

"Go to bed!" Elzire ordered when the dishes were put away.

"Good night, Mom," Yvonne muttered as she left the kitchen.

"Don't you give your mother a kiss any more?" Elzire asked reproachfully.

Yvonne brushed her mother's cheek with her lips and mechanically repeated her good night.

"Sleep well," her mother responded in a neutral tone, as if nothing had happened.

At the top of the stairs, Yvonne came upon Simone comforting Émilie and Marie, who were still crying. She was drying their cheeks with a handkerchief and saying, "It's no big deal, forget about it. She's like that, we can't change her."

Yvonne didn't know what to make of her sister, who was almost fourteen. Their relationship was tense. A great rivalry existed between the quints and Simone and Lucie. The two older sisters often ganged up against Yvonne, who wouldn't back down. Envious and quarrelsome, Simone never missed an opportunity to mock and tease the quints and to accuse them of things that they had not done. Finally, Annette dubbed her "Viper Tongue." Nevertheless, the same Simone had taken great care of Yvonne and Cécile when each had stuck the tines of a pitchfork in her foot. And she was the one who comforted the quints when their mother punished them unjustly and looked after them when they were sick.

"Did she hit you?" Simone asked Yvonne as she approached them.

Yvonne nodded and shrugged helplessly. "Why don't you talk to her, Simone?" she asked. "Mom trusts you. She would listen to you."

"It wouldn't do any good, she doesn't listen to anyone. Except the old man."

"You could try," Yvonne insisted. "You never know."

"No!"

Her refusal was curt and final. The two girls stared at each other coldly for a few seconds. Yvonne realized that it was every man for himself in this house. The undeniable influence that Simone had with their mother would never be used to help the others.

"Come on," Yvonne said to the other quints.

As they went to their rooms, Yvonne told herself that they were on their own; no one would ever take their side.

• • •

A cry awoke Yvonne. It came from nearby.

"Émilie?"

She was lying on her back, completely still.

Yvonne sat up in bed. It had to be morning, since a strong light was filtering through the curtains. She turned her head toward her sister and noticed that her face was unusually pale. Her eyes were wide open.

"Émilie?" Yvonne was worried.

She got up, went to her sister, and leaned over her.

Émilie's eyes were rolled back and staring blankly. Her cheeks seemed to be turning blue. Yvonne touched her arm. Her muscles were taut, as though she were lifting a heavy object. Yvonne slapped her to wake her up.

"Émilie! Émilie!"

No reaction. Yvonne ran to get her sisters. Since they had arrived in the big house, they had been afflicted with illnesses that were usually suffered only by babies and very young children. The family's physician, Dr. Joyal, said that it was because they had lived in isolation and hadn't developed immune defenses.

Marie, Annette, and Cécile rushed to Émilie's bedside, hoping to take care of her without disturbing the rest of the family. Playing doctor and nurse had been their favorite pastime at the hospital, and they routinely gave each other first aid when one had a small injury or a cold.

Émilie's almost black face and violent shaking terrified them.

"Fever?" asked Marie, realizing immediately that this made no sense.

All four ran out into the hall to knock at the door of their parents' bedroom. Agitated, they all talked at once, and neither Elzire nor Oliva could understand what they were saying. However, the girls were so panicked that they knew something serious had happened.

Woken by the commotion, Rachel, Simone, and Lucie followed the others into Émilie's room. Émilie was having violent convulsions and a bloody foam was coming out of her twisted mouth. Elzire quickly recoiled, holding her head in her hands.

"My God!" she exclaimed, horrified. "The grand mal!"

The children had never heard this term. Terrified, they all moved back.

56

For several minutes, the seven girls and their parents were frozen to the spot. Then, overcoming their fear, Yvonne, Annette, Marie, and Cécile went to their sister's bedside.

"We have to call the doctor!" Cécile implored.

Like her sisters, she desperately wanted to take Émilie's suffering for herself, to divide it into five parts so it would be less awful.

"Yes, the doctor," agreed Yvonne.

These words jolted Elzire from her lethargy.

"Keep her from biting her tongue," she told Oliva.

"No. Do it yourself."

He seemed disgusted, but he knew that his wife was paralyzed with fright. When he saw Annette leaning over Émilie, he decided to act. One knee on the bed, he yelled to Simone, who was standing in the doorway, "Go get a spoon."

"What kind?"

"A spoon is a spoon, stupid!" he spat in English.

"There's one in my bathroom," Elzire said to her daughter.

"Why aren't you calling the doctor?" asked Annette impatiently.

Rachel touched her mother's arm. "She's right. Do you want me to call Dr. Joyal?"

Elzire and Oliva, who was forcing Émilie's jaw open, exchanged a look, then Elzire answered, "Yes, but say only that she's sick, no details."

Gradually, Émilie's tremors got less violent and farther apart. She seemed to be in a deep sleep; she was breathing heavily and didn't react when Cécile washed her face, which was beginning to regain its normal color. Elzire picked up the blankets that had fallen on the floor and tucked them in around her daughter.

"Now, no one will know anything happened. Leave her to rest."

The quints would have preferred to stay in their sister's room, but their mother ordered them to go downstairs with the others.

The whole family was in the kitchen, and Elzire made coffee. Disappointed to have missed the show, the boys peppered Lucie and Simone with questions.

"What's 'grand mal,' Mom?" asked Annette in a small voice.

"Epilepsy."

The word meant nothing to the quints. To reassure herself, Marie said confidently, "Dr. Joyal will cure her."

"They can't cure this sickness," Oliva told her. "Émilie will always have attacks like that."

The quints looked at each other, stunned. Yvonne couldn't believe it.

"Always? Are you sure, Dad?"

"If I say it's true, it's true."

"Maybe the doctor . . ."

She stopped as her father shot her a cold glance. He banged his hand on the edge of the sink and looked severely at all the children. "Listen to me, all of you. Not a word of this to anyone, not the doctor, or the nuns. You understand? If this ever gets out of this house, there'll be hell to pay . . ."

The threat didn't need to be made more specific. All the children nodded. Elzire added, "If anyone found out about this, I would be so ashamed! A sickness like this hurts a family's reputation. We've drawn enough attention already. And you'd all have trouble finding husbands if anyone knew."

Like Oliva, Elzire stared coldly at the quints as she talked. The warning was addressed particularly to them. But how did Émilie fit into all of this?

"We have to do something for her," Yvonne begged her father.

After thinking for a couple of moments, he said, "There's no question of going to North Bay. I'll send her to a hospital in Montreal; that way, no one will know. But it won't make much difference."

"They can't cure the grand mal in Montreal or anywhere else. Period, end of story," Elzire concluded, knowing that she wouldn't change her husband's mind.

"What will happen to Émilie if she isn't cured?"

Elzire was annoyed that Cécile was still asking questions after she had closed the discussion.

Oliva shrugged. "Nothing. She'll have the fits regularly. There's nothing to get upset about, it's never more serious than what just happened."

"Can't we help her?"

"Did you see what I did? Put the handle of the spoon in her mouth so she doesn't bite her tongue. The next time she has a fit, do the same thing. And make sure she doesn't hurt herself when she thrashes around. You don't have to come and get me or your mother."

He turned toward Armand, who had put on his coat to go milk the cows. "Take the key and go open the gate for Dr. Joyal."

• • •

The doctor, to whom no one had described Émilie's symptoms, concluded that she had simply fainted. As he left, he whispered to Elzire, "She's started to have her periods."

Marie heard what the doctor said, but she didn't know what it meant, nor did the other quints, to whom she repeated his words. Why had he whispered, as if it were a secret? Maybe it had something to do with the epilepsy.

In the green bedroom, Yvonne, Marie, Annette, and Cécile sat and waited for their sister to wake up. When she opened her eyes, Émilie was surprised to see them all there. She didn't remember anything.

"How do you feel?" Yvonne asked her.

"I ache all over — my back, my arms, my legs — as if I'd been working hard."

"You didn't feel that . . . that . . ."

Yvonne didn't know how to formulate the question. She looked at Cécile, Annette, and Marie to get their approval. There were no secrets among them, so they told Émilie what had happened to her. They tried not to scare her too much, but she was dumfounded. And then she had the unpleasant feeling of being inhabited by something foreign, something she couldn't control, which could attack her at any moment. According to her father, it would happen again.

"And what did the doctor say?" she asked, frightened.

"Dad and Mom didn't want to tell him," said Annette angrily.

"What's going to happen to me?"

"We'll take care of you," her sisters said reassuringly. "Don't worry, we'll take care of you."

"There have been miracles in our lives before," Cécile declared with a conviction that she didn't feel.

But Émilie saw that her sisters were as upset as she was. She didn't want them to make a fuss over her. Smiling, she said, "As long as you're with me, I won't be scared. I know nothing will happen to me."

Behind her back, Yvonne was holding the spoon that she would keep from then on in the drawer of the night table between her bed and Émilie's.

3

"Oh, turn off that damn boring music!" said Lucie, exasperated.

"But it's Chopin," Marie protested.

"I don't care. It's putting me to sleep."

"You never want to listen to anything but country and western," Yvonne retorted.

Aggressively, Lucie looked Yvonne up and down; Yvonne stared back, her face a picture of defiance. To keep things from getting worse, Cécile hurriedly turned off the phonograph.

The rivalry that existed between Yvonne and her sisters Lucie and Simone had only gotten worse in the three and a half years that they had been living under one roof. The rivalry was fueled by their mother, who made the two older girls jealous by saying that Yvonne was Oliva's favorite. Hardheaded Yvonne dealt with the situation as best she could, knowing that the fighting made her sisters unhappy.

Cécile sat down at the table with the other quints and

Lucie. As often happened, they were having supper in the basement playroom — puffed rice, cookies, and milk, while the rest of the family was served meat and vegetables. They were told that cooking for fourteen was sometimes too much work for Elzire. The quints wondered if it wasn't really punishment for having unknowingly broken one of the many unspoken rules in the house.

Being excluded from the dinner table, sometimes with Lucie, didn't really seem like punishment, because it provided a rare opportunity to be alone with each other. Away from their mother's watchful eye, they could laugh and joke without hearing her nag at them to be quiet. After they ate, they sometimes had time to put Strauss waltzes on the phonograph and dance around the room.

"I wonder if the nuns will hold a party to celebrate the end of elementary school," Cécile said to Lucie.

"I'll celebrate when I get away from here. Seven years seeing the same faces is enough!"

The quints were aware that "the same faces" included them.

"I'd rather have gone to school in the village," Lucie continued, "with real people. When I leave this houseful of crazies for boarding school, I won't look back!"

Cécile was thinking exactly the same thing, but she didn't dare express it in those terms; she simply nodded in agreement. This was the best policy with Lucie: to go along with her when what she said was inconsequential, and to try to reason with her when she got carried away. Both in the playground and in the house, Cécile kept Lucie busy to keep her from being mean to the other quints or setting a trap to get them in trouble.

At school, the principal was suspicious of Cécile and treated her more strictly. This nun didn't get along with

Oliva and Elzire, who were paying for the school and often found fault with the education it offered. She thought that Cécile must be close to her parents because she was always with Lucie, so she gave her a particularly hard time.

Cécile also wanted to go away for high school, preferably by herself. Away from her sisters, she would no longer be one of the quintuplets — she'd be a girl like the others, a unique being. She couldn't imagine how that might feel, but surely it would be marvelous. She'd been waiting for this moment for three and a half years. So many times she'd been disheartened, thinking it would never come!

Far from improving, the atmosphere in the big house had steadily worsened over the years. Their father seemed more and more disappointed, their mother more and more bitter. Elzire cried often and spoke badly of Oliva when he wasn't there, reporting to the quints all the terrible things he had said about them, and Oliva was the same way. Another boy had been born into the family the year before. Now, Elzire and Oliva had separate bedrooms, but that did not diminish the tensions between them — quite the contrary.

As the months went by, Cécile and her sisters lost their spirit of initiative and all sense of joy. They saw no one outside of the family circle. They had become friends with the three children of the school janitor, but Lucie had told Oliva and Elzire that the quints were saying bad things about the Dionne family, and the janitor had quickly been replaced by a couple who had only a baby.

Obliged to clean their plates and to drink great quantities of milk, the quints had gotten plump. Elzire chose their clothing without consulting them: identical dresses, too large, with loud patterns that did not suit them. But it was better than going to the Eaton's and Woolworth stores in North Bay, escorted by policemen on motorcycles. The quints got no pleasure from these outings, since the curious crowded around them, shamelessly staring. In any case, going shopping gave them no greater control over what they wore.

"The dishes!" Roger called from the top of the staircase.

"We'll take care of it," Yvonne told Émilie. "You tidy up here a little."

Since she had had her first epileptic seizure, her sisters did everything they could to keep Émilie from doing housework. Marie, who was full of energy despite her small size, often did enough for two. Émilie now had seizures every week, usually after one of the noisy fights that punctuated daily life in the household. Her sisters had learned to take care of her without any help.

"Can you help me, Cécile?" Émilie asked.

Cécile was surprised. Her sister didn't usually ask for help; usually, they had to hold her back. And there were just six bowls, six spoons, and six glasses to wash downstairs — no pots or pans.

"Are you all right, Émilie?" she asked, once they were alone.

"I wanted to talk to you."

They took the place mats into the adjacent small kitchen. Cécile touched her sister's shoulder. "What's the matter?"

"School's almost over here . . . I'm scared they'll put me in reform school."

"Come on, Émilie, you know very well that can't happen."

"Mom said it to me again this morning."

65

"Don't believe her. She knows it scares you and she likes that."

"You think so?"

"Look, they're already hiding your sickness from everyone. Imagine how much more ashamed they'd be if everyone knew there was a Dionne, one of the quints, in one of those places."

The argument made sense to Émilie. She nodded in agreement, but she still looked worried. Cécile knew there was something else she wanted to say.

"What's really bothering you?"

Émilie sighed and hung her head. "It's Roger . . ."

"Uh-oh," groaned Cécile, who immediately understood.

"He comes and lies on top of me and . . . rubs himself."

"Oh, God!"

The news infuriated Cécile, but it didn't surprise her. Roger was very forward. Among themselves, the quints called him "sensual," their euphemism for "lecherous." Not only was he constantly trying to spy on them while they were undressing, as did their other brothers, but he also never missed an opportunity to catch them unawares and grab their private parts.

"Don't let him do it, Émilie."

"He's stronger than me."

It was useless, Cécile knew, to ask their parents to do something. They loved Roger and always made excuses for him. They would accuse Émilie of being provocative, and she would bear the brunt of their reprimands, if not their blows. Cécile could see no solution, and she felt utterly helpless.

No one could come to their rescue. When they had told the nuns about what was going on at the house, the nuns had recommended resignation, love of their parents, and

66

prayer. There was no question of them interceding. Like everyone, they feared Oliva Dionne's reaction.

Cécile tried to sound reassuring. "We'll all keep an eye out for him. But Émilie, make sure you never take off your underpants!"

• • •

"Annette, the toilets!" Elzire shouted, once the dishes were washed.

"Yes, Mom."

Resigned to the unpleasant task, Annette picked up a pail, a rag, and some cleanser. With great difficulty, she repressed her desire to cry out, "Why always me? The others use the toilets, too! Why not Simone or Lucie? Why not the boys?"

"Polish the chrome taps well and don't leave any rings in the bowl like last time."

Annette didn't answer back, even though everything had been spotless the last time. She did everything she could to satisfy her mother, and never got a word of appreciation or thanks — Elzire always found something to criticize. Seven bathrooms to clean, every evening! A chore that took a good two hours and disgusted Annette. And right after she ate! Two hours with her gorge rising. And this chore left her no time to do her homework or study before bedtime at nine o'clock.

The more she did, the more her mother asked of her. Unlike her sisters, she never got a moment's rest. From the moment she got home from school, off to work! They had to get up at six-thirty in the morning in order to have a half hour to practice piano on the family's three instruments. They were watched to make sure they were always busy; if their father and mother weren't home, a

67

brother or sister kept an eye on them in order to report any idleness to their parents.

If it had only been washing dishes, it might not have been so bad, but they also had to make the beds, set the table, sweep, clean the floors, polish the furniture, wash the windows — and then start all over again. Since they had come home, the other children did less, and it was worse now that the two eldest were at boarding school. Weeding the garden or working in the fields became a pleasure, since it allowed them to escape the stifling walls of the house.

Leaving the bathroom near the boys' rooms, Annette ran into her mother, who was coming to inspect. When Elzire lifted her hand to turn on the light, Annette jumped back. Any sudden or unexpected movement by her mother put her on her guard: the slaps came so quickly!

In fact, Annette was Elzire's favorite quintuplet — not because she had a sense of humor and laughed easily (these were qualities that her mother had never appreciated) but simply because she worked without complaining. On rare occasions, when Oliva was away, Annette felt that her mother unlocked her heart and let a bit of happiness out. She wondered why it wasn't always like this. One time, their father had taken the other quints to the dentist in Ottawa. While they spent the afternoon cleaning the house, Annette had seen her mother laugh. Elzire seemed happy to listen to her daughter's stories and songs. For a few hours, Annette thought that everything had changed, that her mother had finally revealed her soft side. Then, Elzire's mood had abruptly clouded over and she'd ordered Annette to go to bed — without supper, even though all the hard work had given her an appetite. Annette could never figure out why her mood had changed so suddenly.

• • •

"Nine o'clock. Good night!" With these words, Elzire curtly announced to the quints, sitting at the dining-room table doing their homework, that it was time for bed.

What about the others? Annette wondered. *They go to bed whenever they like, they do whatever they like. They're allowed to drink coffee, but not us. Too bad Maxwell House doesn't do anything to improve their characters.* She always found a way to make things funny, even the bullying, and her sense of humor was a great help to her sisters in bearing the many annoyances of living in the Dionne household.

"You, Annette. I have something to say to you!"

The imperious tone was not the one that Elzire used to criticize the way a chore had been done. Her sisters gave Annette a questioning look, and she rapidly examined her conscience. She had done nothing wrong.

She followed her mother into the den, which she had transformed into a sewing room.

"Close the door."

Annette did so, then stood before her mother, prudently out of reach.

"Do you write regularly in your diary?"

"Every day, Mom."

That diary! Yet another chore. Elzire had decided that the quintuplets could become writers; to get them in the habit of writing, she required each to keep a diary. And yet there was nothing to fill the pages with except a repetitive account of daily life.

Suddenly, Elzire exploded. "You should be ashamed!" she shouted.

"Of what, Mom?" Annette asked, her voice trembling.

Elzire's face went purple. "Of writing filthy things. And of doing filthy things. I read that you were rubbing Bichonne's tits. You little pervert, admit it!"

Annette was stunned. It had never occurred to her that her mother might read her diary, which she kept in a drawer in her bureau. It was supposed to be personal. Bichonne had had puppies and Annette, intrigued by the dog's swollen teats, had touched them.

"It's not a sin," she protested.

"If I tell you it's wicked, it's wicked!"

"It's no worse than touching the cows' teats, it seems to me . . ."

"Enough back talk!" Elzire shouted, beside herself. "Do you want me to tell your father you're a pervert?"

Flushed with anger, Annette said, "It's not true!"

"Liar. And I know you touch yourself."

"What?"

"You heard me."

"It's not true, Mom," Annette said tearfully.

It seemed that Elzire was enjoying the sight of her daughter squirming with embarrassment.

"Did a nurse tell you to do that? That's what happens when you're reared by strangers. Unless you got it from your father . . . And do your sisters do it, too?"

"No, Mom, you have no right to say that."

"I have a right to say whatever I want. I am your mother. This is my house, and I'm the boss here. And I'm telling you you're a dirty pig!"

Annette bowed her head, knowing it was useless to argue. She stared fixedly at her mother's hands, ready to spring back.

"Go to bed. I've seen enough of you for one day. And

remember, I know everything. You can't hide anything from me."

Annette swallowed her anger and ran upstairs. She had never been so ashamed in her life! Quickly, to sleep, to oblivion!

She found Cécile writing in her diary, stretched out on her stomach on her bed. The radio on the night table was playing soft music.

"If you ever have something important to tell Mom and you want to be sure she hears you," Annette announced, her voice dripping with sarcasm, "just write it in your diary."

"I don't understand," said Cécile, closing her diary.

"She reads what we write!"

"Really?"

Annette sat on the edge of Cécile's bed and told her what her mother had just done — though she didn't mention the part about the "touching," a story she would save for another time.

"Poor Annette, you should have been more careful. She opens all the letters we get, you know that. We have nothing of our own here. We're strangers, they tell us so often enough, and that's what we'll always be."

"If it were just me, I would have been gone long ago."

"What do you mean?"

Annette leaned over to her sister and whispered, "Do you daydream at night before you sleep?"

"No."

"So, what do you think about?"

"About getting to sleep as quick as I can!"

After a moment of hesitation, Annette began again, still whispering, "You know how much I love all of you . . ."

"You don't even have to say it."

"Well, every night, I dream about escaping from here. I see myself going downstairs at night, without making a sound. I take the key in the kitchen and I go outside. I talk softly to the dogs so they won't bark. I go to the fence, open the lock, and there I am, on the road."

"All alone?"

"Yes," Annette answered, woefully. "Other times, the key isn't there, so I climb the fence, throw my suitcase over to the other side, and I go over the barbed wire, trying not to hurt myself. And I get out to the road."

"What happens once you're on the road?"

Annette sighed deeply. "Nothing. I don't know what to do. That's why I start the plan again every night — to try to figure out what to do next, where to go."

"It's understandable. We have no money, we don't know anyone, we wouldn't know how to get along in the world. I wouldn't know how to help you. So it's better that it stay a dream, Annette."

"Why?"

"If you escape, they'll find you, and it'll be you, not Émilie, who'll wind up in reform school!"

They giggled, their hands in front of their mouths to stifle the sound. They didn't believe the threat their mother used to terrorize Émilie. Better not to take it seriously — that would take the sting out of it.

The brief moment of hilarity over, Annette got serious again. "I'm unhappy, Cécile."

Her sister gave her a hug. "We all are, Annette."

"I'm depressed. I can't take it any more. Myself, I can always get by. But I can't stand seeing how they treat our little Marie and our poor Émilie."

"Keep your chin up. Things will change. There's no high school in the area, so they'll have to send us to boarding school, like Simone and Rachel. Just four months more. And summer isn't quite so bad. We can go outside."

"I'd like to go away and never come back," Annette murmured with a faraway look.

After a moment of silence, her eyes suddenly lit up with an amusing thought. She smiled. "At seven toilets per day, how many until September?"

• • •

Named "Mother of the Year" in 1947, Elzire Dionne went to Ottawa to attend the ceremony. Simone and Lucie went with her. Because all five had whooping cough, the quints stayed home. But that was just an excuse; if they hadn't been sick, their mother would have found another good reason not to take them. It was better this way; if they'd gone, they would probably have been on exhibit, like animals at a fair. And they would have had their mother on their backs the entire trip: "Don't do this! Don't do that! Stand up straight!"

In Elzire's absence, their father was more relaxed, not as strict, and a little less distant. He didn't even comment when he found all five of them in the same room when he got home from North Bay one day.

"How are my little girls?" he asked gently as he came into the room. "Have you taken your syrup?"

"Yes, Dad," they responded in unison.

They had been sick for three weeks, and they were feeling better every day. The coughing bouts were farther apart and less wracking.

"I have a surprise for you," Oliva said, holding out a box he'd been hiding behind his back.

Chocolates! It was the first time he had given them

something for no reason at all, without a camera there to witness it. The gesture touched them deeply, and they thanked him warmly.

"Do you want some, Dad?" Émilie asked as she unwrapped the box.

"No, thanks. Keep them for yourselves. And don't tell anyone, especially your mother. Make sure she doesn't find the box when she gets back from Ottawa."

"Promise," said Marie.

"What did you do this afternoon?" Oliva asked Yvonne.

"Not much. We took a nap. Oh, yes . . . Sister Aimée-des-Anges came to see us."

His teeth clenched, Oliva's lips twitched involuntarily with annoyance.

"What did she want?"

"Nothing, Dad," Cécile said, trying to minimize the event. "Just to find out how we were doing."

"If she wanted to know, she could have called me."

"She thought we might go back to school this week," Marie said.

Oliva groaned and raised his voice. "Why is she sticking her nose in where it doesn't belong? I'm the one who decides. I'm going to give her a piece of my mind."

Émilie worried that their father's irritation would boil over into a full-fledged rage. Suddenly, a coughing fit overtook her, and she had trouble catching her breath. She went into the bathroom to spit up the phlegm that filled her mouth. At least she wasn't vomiting as she had in previous weeks. When she came back, Oliva asked, in a soft voice, "Are you all right?"

Thanks to this interruption, he had regained his temper. Annette wanted to cheer her father up and bring back the smile he'd had a few minutes before.

74

"I think Sister Aimée-des-Anges is already feeling sad that she won't be seeing us next autumn."

Oliva just nodded distractedly.

Yvonne thought this might be a good time to bring up the subject she had been discussing with her sisters for weeks. Such an opportunity did not present itself often. "In fact, Dad . . . next autumn . . ."

"Yes?" he said, suddenly on his guard.

"We'd like to go to boarding school, like Rachel and Simone. Like Armand."

He looked thoughtful for a few seconds before answering. "I've considered it. I'm still thinking about it. My concern is that you'll be kidnapped. You're famous, and people think I'm rich."

"If each of us was in a different school," Cécile pointed out, "there wouldn't be any danger."

Annette added, "We could even change our name. No one would know we were the quints."

This suggestion displeased Oliva. He stared at her, frowning. "You'd agree to be separated?" he thundered.

They all nodded.

"Education is very important," Yvonne said, "if you want to get ahead in life."

"And what would you like to be when you grow up?"

"A nurse."

"That's no profession, wiping the brow of sick people," he said, annoyed. "Besides, the nurses I've known have not been very nice people. But never mind, we'll discuss this another time."

The subject, which he felt he had closed with his last pronouncement, had bothered Oliva. He could see now that the plans he had for the future of his little girls might never be realized, simply because they weren't aware of

75

how famous they really were. Instead of dreaming, like other young girls, of being celebrated actresses or winning acclaim in other professions, all they wanted was anonymity, to be women just like other women. *A nurse, huh!*

"It's all very well and good to want an education," he continued, "but you have to have the means."

"It's true that putting five girls through school is expensive," Marie conceded.

"That's not the problem. It's a question of intelligence."

"We do well in school," Yvonne protested.

"You're just in elementary school, and you have private teachers. Since I'm the one who pays them, it would be stupid of them to give you low marks."

Deeply wounded by their father's words, the quints bowed their heads and said nothing.

"You have narrow, low foreheads," he told them. "Look at Roger, with his wide, high forehead. That's a sign of intelligence. He's much smarter than you."

Yvonne's temper rose. Roger, always Roger. Why did he have to denigrate them to make Roger look good? She gripped the box of chocolates more tightly, though the contents interested her less now.

Cécile saw what her sister was feeling and took up the argument, concealing her own chagrin.

"We'll work harder than the others if we have to, but we'll succeed in our studies, Dad."

"Well . . . you'll study, we'll see what that does. All my children will have the same chances in life, even if some are not gifted by nature. So, time for bed."

"About boarding school, Dad?" Cécile insisted as he headed for the door.

"Leave that to me."

Once they were alone, Marie grabbed the box and hastily unwrapped it. Before taking a chocolate, she offered the box around to her sisters.

Yvonne refused. "Not right away. I feel a little sick to my stomach."

This reminded the others of what their father had said about their intelligence.

"I guess I'll wait too," Marie said, putting down the box.

She thought for a few moments about what her father had said, then declared, "It's not true! We're just as smart as the others."

"Yes, and smarter than some," Yvonne added. "Right, Cécile?"

Standing in front of the mirror on her bureau, Cécile had lifted her bangs to look at her forehead.

"Pull your hair back," Annette teased her. "It'll make your forehead higher!"

But Cécile didn't laugh as she looked at her sisters in the mirror. Her voice trembled with emotion. "Still, it hurts . . ."

The others were silent, recognizing in their sister the very feeling that they were trying to bury. Finally, Yvonne said, "At least we know we'll be going back to school."

"For a moment," Annette admitted, "I was worried he'd say we have to stay home as servants and cleaning women!"

"You think we'll really go to boarding school?" asked Émilie hopefully.

"You heard him — the same thing for all the children," Cécile answered. "The older ones are in boarding school."

"I'll believe it the day I leave with my suitcase," said Annette, worn down by too many disappointments. "Not before."

• • •

Yvonne and Émilie jumped at the sound of someone knocking at their door. Since the radio was playing, they hadn't heard any noises from the hall. Yvonne hurriedly swallowed the chocolate in her mouth and signaled to her sister to hide the box. As she wiped her lips with the inside of her sleeve, she said, "Come in."

The door opened. It was their father.

"Why didn't you answer right away when I knocked?"

"I was swallowing my chocolate," she answered, laughing.

Sharing a secret with her father made her happy. It was sweet revenge on the brothers and sisters who always knew everything before the quints did. Émilie was also pleased, and showed him the box, which she had hidden under her pillow.

"They're very good, Dad. Do you want one?"

He took one and ate it, smiling at the girls.

"You're still coughing. I heard you when I was at the door."

"A little," Émilie admitted, "but it's much better."

"Whooping cough can be dangerous. You must be sure to take care of yourselves."

Yvonne had noticed a change in attitude in their father. Never had he shown such concern for them, nor had he ever talked to them so kindly. And in the days leading up to her trip to Ottawa, their mother, too, had been gentler with them. Could it be that the miracle was happening at last, after almost four years? Could the respect and obedience that they had shown to their parents finally have put a spark of love in their hearts?

Perhaps the others had complained of having to do too

78

much work while they were sick, and their mother and father had realized exactly how much housework the quints did every day; maybe their parents had realized that the girls did more than was possible and deserved some respect. Or maybe it was their looming departure for boarding school that had brought some appreciation. It would have been better if it had happened long ago, but better late than never.

Oliva sat on the edge of Yvonne's bed and showed her a brown bottle.

"This liniment is excellent for chest colds."

"Thanks, Dad."

Yvonne reached out for the bottle, but he moved it beyond her grasp.

"I'll rub you down myself."

She couldn't believe her ears. And yet her father was saying, insistently, "It's for your own good. Take off your pajama top."

Yvonne shot an incredulous look at Émilie, who was dumfounded and red-faced with shame. Her own cheeks, too, must have been scarlet; she could feel them burning.

Oliva thundered, teasingly, "Are you shy in front of your own father? Come on, now! I only want to see you healthy."

"But, Dad . . ." Yvonne stuttered.

Her father's face hardened and his voice took on its familiar authoritarian tone. "Stop being so childish, take off your top! I don't have all the time in the world."

Yvonne told herself that he didn't realize that she was modest, and all he wanted to do was take care of his daughters. She felt guilty for misinterpreting his gesture of goodwill: she was seeing evil when he was only showing compassion. After all, she undressed in front of Dr. Joyal when he examined her. To avoid embarrassment, she could simply look away while he rubbed her chest.

Not meeting her father's eye, Yvonne unbuttoned her pajama top, opened it, and sat with her face to the wall. She heard him unscrew the top of the bottle and pour the liniment onto his hand. She tried to empty her mind, but she couldn't keep herself from thinking that her breasts were bare, that he could rub his hand right near them. Why this terrible anxiety? Why could she not find this normal? Could this be what the nuns called "morbid irresolution"?

Damp hands were placed at the base of her neck and slid toward her shoulders, exerting pressure. An aroma of herbal infusion filled Yvonne's nose as the hands went over and over the same spots. The medication penetrated her skin, producing a sensation of heat. The hands moved downward, and the fingers met at the sternum and spread to rub her ribs. *Let it be over quickly!*

"You'll see, this'll do you good."

He put more liniment on his hands and rubbed her skin in larger circles. Did he know that his palms were brushing the edge of her breasts every time they moved? Was it by mistake?

"Feels good, eh?"

She didn't answer; she kept staring at the wall. His voice was sharper than usual, almost nervous. His breathing was rapid and noisy. As his fingers wandered around her breasts, massaging them, Yvonne realized that her father was deriving pleasure from applying the liniment. He was drawing out the procedure much longer than necessary. Even though she was disgusted and wished she were somewhere else, she didn't dare protest. She had never been so ashamed in all her life. Quickly, she closed her eyes when her glance met her sister's. Since Oliva's back was to Émilie, she didn't see the strange look on his face or the way his hands were moving on Yvonne's breasts.

The rubbing turned into caressing. It was becoming disgusting instead of just unpleasant. Yvonne suddenly felt nauseated. She shivered.

"I'm getting cold," she said, turning to her father.

His eyes were bright as he smiled at his daughter. But when she crossed the sleeves of her pajama top over her chest, his smile disappeared. He withdrew his hands without further ado. She hastily buttoned her top while he went to the neighboring bed, then she pulled the covers up to her neck.

"Your turn, Émilie."

Émilie opened her top without protesting. Of course, she was scarlet and she trembled when Oliva's hands touched her.

Yvonne would have liked to lose herself in sleep to forget what had just happened, but she had to keep watch over her sister. Lying on her back, Yvonne pretended to gaze at the ceiling, but out of the corner of her eye she watched her father's movements. Especially his face. He stared unabashedly at Émilie's breasts, since she had closed her eyes. It quickly became obvious to Yvonne that it gave him great pleasure to touch his daughters' chests.

Liniment rubs? An excuse to see their bare breasts. Suddenly, a fact that until then had seemed harmless took on a whole new meaning for Yvonne. When Dr. Joyal came to see them, the examinations always took place in Oliva's office, with him right there. Yvonne had thought that her father was merely lacking in civility, but now, she knew that he'd been getting an eyeful! Like he was doing right now. Never again would she feel at ease with him; when he looked at her, she would never again believe that it was a father's innocent look. Roger was just following in his father's footsteps!

An aggravating thought occurred to her: what about that time when Émilie had been surprised by a face at the window when she was taking a bath, a face that had disappeared too quickly for her to identify it? Yvonne and Lucie had rushed outside and found the big ladder still leaning against the wall, just under the bathroom window. No one was around. They'd looked in the boys' rooms; none of them seemed out of breath. As for their father, he'd been in his office, and they hadn't dared push the door open. Oliva had claimed that it was a prowler, but how could a prowler have gotten into the yard, with the locks, the barbed wire, and the two guard dogs?

"It'll make you feel better, you'll see, Émilie. Your cough will go away."

The same high-pitched voice, a little feverish. And Émilie, so innocent and unsuspecting, didn't realize that it wasn't normal. Yvonne quivered with indignation. That man was repugnant. To think, she had believed he was being nicer to them because he was beginning to love them. And the chocolates! Ruses to gain their trust. Had he done this to the older girls as well?

"You must be getting cold, Émilie."

Oliva looked crossly at Yvonne the moment the words were out of her mouth, but she kept talking. "You know, Dad, wet skin makes the whole body feel cold. I think we're still a little under the weather."

He didn't answer, but he withdrew from between the two beds. Yvonne's voice had broken the spell. He picked up his bottle and went to the door.

"Sleep well."

"Thanks, Dad," they replied gloomily.

The door closed. The two girls looked at each other. Yvonne was relieved to see that her sister hadn't been taken in by their father's mock concern. Émilie was as upset and humiliated as she was. How could they prevent him from doing it again? There was no one they could ask for help, no one who could intervene. Yvonne felt totally powerless.

They heard Oliva knocking at Annette and Cécile's bedroom door. Furiously, Yvonne said to Émilie, "It's not right! No, it's not right!"

She felt sullied and wanted to wash her chest, but she might make herself even sicker — and risk attracting more "care" from her father.

"It's not right!" she repeated, defeated.

• • •

Three times a week, the priest from Corbeil came to celebrate mass in the private chapel set up in the old nurses' residence, where the nuns now lived. Elzire was very religious, and she took all the children, except for one quint, who would stay behind to prepare and serve breakfast to Oliva.

All five hated this arrangement, because it meant that they had to cut short their piano practice to be at the altar at seven o'clock. But the one who stayed at home hated it the most, because she'd have to listen to Oliva complaining about his wife. He always said that she was a bad mother, who twisted her babies' feet when they cried, left them for hours in dirty diapers, and so on. They refused to believe these tales, as they refused to believe what their mother told them about their father.

Even more than the arguments and quarrels that broke out regularly between Elzire and Oliva, their eagerness to destroy each other's image bothered the quints. They sensed between their parents no tenderness or pleasure in being together. Each seemed to fear the other. They agreed on nothing except the necessity to keep up appearances in front of strangers.

For Oliva, who had so often been taken to task by the newspapers, public opinion was of the utmost importance. "All those reporters are waiting for," he often said to the quints, "is for one of you to get pregnant." He tried to control what was published about the quintuplets and their family, letting out only the information that he wanted to see in print.

The newspaper clippings that were accumulating in albums testified to his passion for publicity, and he took advantage of the smallest event to keep the Dionne name in the media. When his eldest son, Armand, got married, in the spring of 1947, Oliva decided that the wedding would take place in the private chapel in the old hospital and not in the Corbeil church. The quints were the maids of honor, which drew reporters and photographers. It was also a hunger for publicity that led him to accept, two months later, an invitation to participate in the celebrations of the hundredth anniversary of the foundation of the Ottawa diocese.

The crush of the crowds at this event was distressing for the quints, who were aware as never before of the curiosity they provoked. Every time they went somewhere, the faithful turned out in droves, and it happened

One month after his famous quintuplets were born, Oliva Dionne lost custody of them to the Ontario government. Initially, this arrangement was to last for two years, but it was later decided that guardianship of the quintuplets would last until their eighteenth birthday. Oliva Dionne waged an unremitting battle to reverse this decision. On November 17, 1943, he finally brought his nine-year-old girls home. Everywhere, the papers celebrated this family reunion.

*The Dionne quintuplets grew up before the eyes of hundreds
of thousands of visitors — it is estimated that more than
three million people filed through the observation gallery
of The Dafoe Hospital and Nursery — and under the care of nurses
who tended to them day and night.*

*From the start, the identical character of the quintuplets was emphasized by
identical dresses and hairstyles. This was how the public liked to see the
"princesses of Canada," here preparing to meet King George VI.*

All the quintuplets' achievements and activities were caught on film.
The "Dionne quints" had their appointed photographer, Fred Davis, and later
the photographer they called Mr. Sasse, who continued to visit them once
they were living with their family.

"Quintland," as depicted in Life *magazine. 1. The house where the quintuplets were born. 2. Oliva Dionne's woolens shop. 3. Oliva Dionne's souvenir shop and restaurant. 4. The residence for hospital personnel, which would later become the nuns' residence. 5. The observation gallery and the playground, where visitors could catch a glimpse of the little girls. Later, it became the playground for their school. 6. The Dafoe Hospital and Nursery was converted first into the Dionne family's private school, then into a girls' boarding school, Villa Notre-Dame.*

The new Dionne house, built and furnished at a cost of $90,000, which came from the quints' fund, comprised nineteen rooms, including eight bedrooms and seven bathrooms.

Oliva Dionne purchased his first Cadillac soon after the quintuplets were born. Thereafter, he bought the latest model every year.

*Cécile, Yvonne, Marie, Émilie, and Annette (l. to r.),
now living in the "big house."*

*In their parents' new home, Yvonne (seen in the mirror) and Marie hold their
dolls. Cécile and Annette lived in the "yellow room." The "green room" was
Yvonne and Émilie's. Marie, separated from her sisters for the first time, lived
with one of her other sisters in the "pink room."*

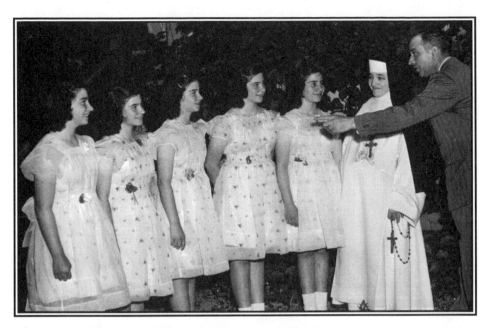

Émilie, Annette, Cécile, Yvonne, and Marie (l. to r.) smile at their father under the tender gaze of an aunt, Sister Ange-du-Bon-Secours.

A few years later, Émilie, Marie, Cécile, Yvonne, and Annette (l. to r.) visited their aunt in the convent where she was living, accompanied by their appointed photographer.

Émilie, Yvonne, Annette, Cécile, and Marie (l. to r.) with the Great Dane named Bichonne and one of her puppies.

When they were thirteen, Cécile, Annette, Émilie, Yvonne, and Marie (l. to r.), along with their parents and Father Sauvé, took part in the celebrations for the hundredth anniversary of the Ottawa diocese.

again when the Dionne family, all dressed up, took their place in the front row of seats set up on the grass for an open-air mass. Marie complained to Father Sauvé, who was accompanying the Dionne family.

"Now, now, Marie," he answered, "don't you know it's because people love you?"

"Love us, Father Sauvé? They don't even know us!"

"That's where you're wrong. They've been following every event in your lives since you were born. You are part of their memories. They feel like they know you very well. The miracle of your birth was a sign of hope for everyone during difficult times."

She frowned, perplexed. "It's no fun having everyone stare at us."

"Tell yourself they're friendly looks. People love you because you've remained simple and friendly. Think of the hundreds of letters you get every month from all over the place, full of good wishes and warm thoughts."

Marie thought for a moment. Friendly looks? She had never thought of it that way; usually, she felt people were trying to find fault with her. And suddenly, the thousands of pairs of eyes from the crowd seemed less frightening. Now she could relax and return to the thoughts that had been preoccupying her and her sisters for months. June was drawing to a close, and they still didn't know what the future held in store for them.

Making sure that her father was still at the other end of the family group, she asked the priest, "Father Sauvé, has Dad told you where we're going to school in September?"

He seemed surprised. "You don't have the slightest idea?"

"No."

"What would you like?"

She sighed. "To go to boarding school."

It was the priest's turn to glance over at Oliva, who, his neck craned, was watching them anxiously. Father Sauvé knew that Oliva didn't trust him and hated to see him speaking privately with one of the quints.

"I think your father has other plans for you."

This muttered sentence made Marie apprehensive all over again. "What plans, Father Sauvé?"

"Well," he started, a little uncomfortable, "if your father hasn't seen fit to tell you, he must have his reasons. I mustn't betray his secrets. Look, here's Monseigneur Mar Ivanios, the archbishop of Trivandrum, in India." And the priest turned away, absorbing himself in the spectacle of the arrival of the princes of the Church.

Marie knew that this was his way of ending the conversation. He felt that he had already said too much, and she would get no more out of him. She stared at the ground. Throughout the ceremony, she tried in vain to decipher Father Sauvé's words, to imagine what her father's plans were.

It was in the *Nugget* that she finally discovered the bad news: they would not be going to boarding school; instead, the boarding school would be coming to them. Their father had gotten permission from the government and the Catholic Church to transform the hospital into a high school. The red-painted wooden building, once an elementary school for all of Oliva's children, would become Villa Notre-Dame, a boarding school for young girls that would continue to be managed by the Sisters of the Assumption.

There would be ten students in addition to the quintuplets. The article quoted Oliva Dionne at length. He said, among other things, "It was impossible to enrol the quintuplets in a regular school. This way, they will be able to continue their studies, as is their wish. They will have the company of girls their own age, which is very normal, without being deprived of the family atmosphere and protection."

"'Family atmosphere!'" exclaimed Annette, with a sarcasm that could not hide her terrible disappointment.

"He could have asked our opinion," said Yvonne, who quickly realized the irony of this remark. They had never been asked their opinion on anything. The parents decided; the girls obeyed.

Marie cried, "It's not fair. Lucie is going away in September. Why not us? It's not fair!"

"Have you ever seen fairness in this house?" retorted Émilie, bitterly. "I haven't!"

Annette discreetly wiped away a tear: her dream of escape, which she had thought was finally within her grasp, was receding irretrievably. They would be condemned to spend the rest of their lives in this house, as servants to their parents.

"As soon as I'm of age," she announced, "I'm entering a convent."

Her sisters knew she wasn't kidding. They all believed that they would never marry, and the idea of becoming nuns often came to mind.

"You're awfully quiet," Yvonne said to Cécile. "What are you thinking?"

"When she mentioned Lucie, Marie gave me an idea. I'll ask Lucie to talk to them. Maybe Dad will listen to her."

"Yes, do that."

"While we're waiting," Émilie said, "we'll pray that it works."

After she told her about their wish to go to boarding

school in a different region, Cécile begged Lucie to inter-
cede with their father.

"What are you complaining about? You're getting a
boarding school just for you!"

"But it's not what we want, you know that, Lucie. We
would love to go away for a bit, like you and Rachel and
Simone. It would do everyone so much good."

"Not Mom and Dad. And I won't talk to them about it."

"Why?"

"Because."

"Do me this one favor, Lucie, I'm begging you."

"I wouldn't have the heart to cause them so much pain.
You have to understand, they were deprived of you five
for so long that now they want to keep you close to them,
even if it is more expensive for the old man than sending
you to a school far away. Make a little effort. They deserve
it. They've suffered so much because of you."

Lucie didn't usually show such consideration for her
parents, and Cécile tried to assess how much irony was
hidden in her words. She asked once more, but this time
Lucie gave a categorical refusal: "No way!"

As Cécile was leaving, crestfallen, Lucie called after her,
"You think the old man would change his mind after it's
been in the papers? What kind of fool would he look like
then?"

4

All summer long, the sound of hammers and saws echoed through the forest around Oliva Dionne's farm: carpenters were busy making changes to the old hospital, adding a dormitory, among other things. The cost of renovating and operating Villa Notre-Dame would be $70,000, which would be taken from the quintuplets' fund.

After their initial disappointment, the quints got used to the idea of returning to live in the building where they had spent a happy childhood. Of course, they wouldn't leave the compound, and they would remain within shouting distance of the big house and under the watchful eye of their parents, but still, it was an improvement. No more domestic chores, no more of the incessant quarrels. They wouldn't go to the big house except to visit — as infrequently as possible, they hoped.

As September approached, time seemed to stand still. The workers' banging became sweet music to their ears. As they played in the yard or weeded the garden, they could see the red-painted wooden building, and they tried to figure out how far along the construction was. There was no question of their going over to see; their father had explicitly forbidden them to approach the strangers working there.

When cars stopped in front of the gate, as they did several times a day during the summer, the quints had to go inside the house, out of sight of the curious. However, in spite of their timidity, they were eager to see new faces, to communicate with people who would broaden their horizons. It was precisely against this that their father warned them every day.

Not just anyone could come into the big house. Only Oliva's relatives, acquaintances, and trusted guests were allowed in, and he kept an eye on them to make sure they didn't have private conversations with any of the quintuplets. He or Elzire personally went through the many letters from admirers that arrived each week.

Finally, it was the first day of school! Yvonne, Annette, Émilie, Marie, and Cécile went downstairs, each carrying a little suitcase. Three trunks had preceded them into the boarding school; they had no idea why there were only three trunks for the five of them. Émilie prayed over and over to the Virgin Mary that this would not be just a dream, that their father wouldn't change his mind at the last minute.

As for Marie, she was bridling withimpatience. She regretted that she and her sisters hadn't been there to welcome their classmates. They owed them at least that small gesture of politeness, it seemed to her. But their father didn't want the parents who were bringing their daughters to come into contact with his quintuplets. The entire afternoon, the girls had watched cars going through the gate leading to the boarding school, people getting out, and the cars leaving again. As they waited, they developed stage fright: suddenly, the prospect of meeting their ten potential friends all at the same time made them terribly anxious.

Oliva and Elzire were waiting for their daughters at the bottom of the stairs. Their faces betrayed no emotion. Elzire said, flatly, "With eight away in boarding school, the house will seem empty."

It was a simple statement, which, pronounced in another tone of voice, might have suggested that their mother was sad to see them go.

And no more servants to do the housework . . . Marie thought.

"You'll have to be careful," Oliva declared. "We won't be there to protect you all the time. Don't trust the nuns: there might be one rotten apple in the barrel. That happens with nuns and priests. Don't get familiar with them, or with the other girls."

"It's simple," Elzire continued. "You say nothing. What goes on here doesn't concern them. People are as curious as weasels!"

They nodded their heads, in a hurry to go. But their father had not finished his instructions.

"You're smart enough to size things up. Don't believe everything they tell you. They might try to influence you in the wrong way, turn you against your parents, try to divide our family again. If that happens, I want you to tell me right away. I'll take care of it fast!"

This speech surprised the quints, since most of the five nuns were the same ones who'd been teaching them for years.

"Anyway, I'll go over every day to check things out," Oliva concluded. "Now, get going."

• • •

Kneeling on the back seat of the car so she could get a better view, Jacqueline looked curiously at the three buildings that sat along the edge of the gravel road. Painted signs identified them as the midwives' shop and the shops belonging to the father of the Dionne quintuplets.

Her excitement at the idea of going to the same boarding school as the quints, whom the papers talked about so often, had subsided. The place seemed isolated, she thought, and her parents would be going home without her. She would be all alone with strangers.

"You remember when we came when you were six or seven?"

"Yes, Mama," she answered, unenthusiastically.

"There were quite a few more cars that day," her father said. "They were on both sides of the road, and the parking lot was full. We had to park a half mile down."

"But it was worth it," her mother said. "It's one of my favorite memories." She turned toward her daughter. "Do you remember, Jacqueline?"

"Yes," the teenager said distractedly.

How could she forget that visit? She'd looked forward to it for months. She'd felt as though she already knew the quints, who were her age, because her mother had collected everything that was said about them and read her all the newspaper articles. Still fresh in her memory were the hours of waiting under a hot sun, the crowd's excitement, her thirst. With the other visitors, she and her parents had rushed to the observation gallery when the policemen opened the gate. It had been a magical moment, full of intense emotion.

"If they'd told me then," her mother continued, "that

92

one day you would be going to school with them, I never would have believed it!"

Jacqueline, too, had found it hard to believe when the Sisters of the Assumption, who had a school in her village, some sixty miles away, had chosen her as a classmate for the famous quintuplets.

"It must be this gate," said her father, stopping before the red building that had once been called The Dafoe Hospital and Nursery.

A young man guarding the entrance checked the identity of the visitors, then let them in.

"Probably one of their brothers," her father said, once their car window was closed again. "Not very talkative! I hope the quints aren't too snobbish. If things don't work out, Jacky, call us. We'll come and get you."

"Snobs? Come on," his wife scolded him. "They're charming and very simple, everyone knows it. I'm sure they'll like our Jacqueline."

The girl, nervous, said nothing. She had been looking forward to this day, but she hadn't guessed that she would be so impressed, or that it would be so hard to leave her parents for the first time. Her throat tight, she glanced at the girls who were talking with the nuns outside the school, realizing, with disappointment, that the Dionne quints weren't among them.

Once her trunk was inside and her parents had gone, Jacqueline found herself at loose ends, her heart heavy. Not knowing anyone, she stood apart from the group.

• • •

Excitement overtook the quints as they approached Villa Notre-Dame, but they didn't let it show. They were sure that their father, who was with them, would resent it. A

93

little superstitious, Émilie resisted the temptation to look over her shoulder one last time at the big house; she remembered the story of the wife of Lot, who was changed into a pillar of salt for having turned to look back.

Marie stepped off the path, since her father's silhouette blocked her view; she counted nine girls in front of the school and on the porch. Which one would be her best friend? She just had to find a friend who wasn't also one of her sisters.

As they arrived, the quints smiled and nodded at their new classmates, then went to put their things inside. Oliva stayed outside with the principal, who said, "It's a big day, Mr. Dionne. You can be proud of having created a new institution where young girls will be educated in the faith of our Holy Mother Church."

"If you say so," Oliva answered as he observed the girls with a critical eye. "Are they all girls from good families?"

"Absolutely, Mr. Dionne. Our community hand-picked them, in both Quebec and Ontario. They're religious, studious, and serious. They'll be ideal companions for your daughters."

"So now, is everything ready?"

"Not entirely. We can't move into the dormitory until tomorrow. Tonight, the girls will sleep in the drawing room."

"Will someone be staying with them at night?"

The nun took umbrage at the question. "Mr. Dionne," she said pointedly, "you can trust me and my nuns. It is our mission to teach young girls and to watch over them, we're used to it."

"And as their father, it's my duty to be concerned with my daughters' lot. God entrusted them to me."

"Of course. Your solicitude in their regard honors you."

Sister Aimée-des-Anges had learned over the years to deal with this hard, intransigent, sometimes hurtful man. It was always best to leave the last word to him.

The quints came back outside and kissed Oliva on the cheek, as their mother had told them to do. He then walked away down the path toward the big brick house. Émilie felt that a weight had been lifted from her shoulders: now, their new life could really start. They stood with the nuns at the bottom of the small stairway to the porch, not daring to take the first steps toward the other girls, who were also frozen to the spot. When their eyes met, both groups gave timid little smiles. Suddenly, one of the girls began to cry.

Sister Aimée-des-Anges tried to comfort her. "Are you missing your parents already?"

"Yes . . ."

"Now, now, don't worry, it will pass. You're among friends here. Your name is Jacqueline, isn't it?"

"Yes, Sister."

The nun affectionately patted her cheek.

The students had to be kept busy until supper, to give them an opportunity to get to know each other. The nun clapped her hands to get their attention. "Girls! Come over here."

They formed a semicircle around her.

"I greeted you all individually, but I want once again to welcome you into this family that we will make together. There are only fourteen of you, but a fifteenth girl will join us soon. Now, the rules are a little less strict than in a large boarding school. You can speak at meals, in the hallway, and in the dormitory. Not too loudly, of course. Any questions?"

She looked at each girl in turn. Since no one spoke,

she continued. "From now until suppertime, you will form teams of two and review your multiplication tables as you walk the grounds. The exercise will work up an appetite."

She paired the girls off. Reviewing the multiplication tables was just an excuse; the nun was sure that once the girls were alone with each other they would find something else to talk about.

"Annette and Jacqueline, you'll work together."

The two girls started away from the group.

"Where shall we go?" Annette asked.

"Wherever you like."

They began to walk toward the observation gallery. Annette felt feverish: this was the first time she'd ever found herself speaking to a girl her own age who was not a relative, and she didn't know what to do. She wanted so much to make a good impression that she was speechless. Finally, curiosity got the better of her.

"Do you come from a city?"

"A large town."

Not knowing anything about the outside world, Annette quizzed her classmate on her family, friends, previous school, games. Jacqueline realized that Annette was genuinely interested and answered directly. She was amazed to find that this famous girl was no different from herself or her friends. And when she expressed this thought out loud, Annette beamed. She couldn't have imagined a nicer compliment.

The ice was broken. The two girls talked about their tastes and interests, joked, and told each other that they knew their multiplication tables well enough not to have to review them. Without thinking, they found themselves inside the observation gallery, where the stagnant, humid,

96

cool air amplified the dense silence.

Jacqueline recalled her first visit to this gallery: the stifling heat, the heavy scents of body odor and drugstore perfumes, the muffled hubbub of whispered conversations, punctuated from time to time with exclamations. There were women crying; one woman fainted near them. With her father carrying her piggyback, she had avidly watched the five little girls playing in the playground. They were so pretty in their yellow dresses, with matching yellow ribbons in their hair! Three quints were riding around the yard on their tricycles, and the other two were wading in a little swimming pool. The onlookers were delighted. The quints seemed so happy that Jacqueline envied them; she would have liked to play with them.

Jacqueline and Annette walked slowly. On their right, the wall was pierced with windows covered on the outside with a fine metal mesh. They leaned their elbows on a windowsill, contemplating the playground, now invaded by weeds.

"The mesh was so we wouldn't see the visitors," Annette murmured.

"You knew there were people watching you?"

"Not at first. We heard noise, but we didn't know where it came from. Sometimes, we'd see blurry shapes. When we were older, we knew what was going on. Émilie and Marie clowned around to amuse people."

"Didn't it bother you that people were watching you?"

"We were used to it. We didn't know any other way of life, so it was natural for us."

"What was it like to be famous, to have so many people coming to see you, to get your picture taken all the time?"

"Nothing, I guess. It was natural, like the visitors at the

playground. We didn't know there were other ways to live."

"Didn't you feel like prisoners?"

"We were happy." Annette sighed sadly.

Jacqueline stopped talking. She could see that Annette was about to say something important, but a long silence followed.

Then Annette said, suddenly, "Seven times nine?"

"Sixty-three," Jacqueline responded automatically.

They burst out laughing and the look they exchanged was friendly. Already, a bond was forming between them.

"I'm worried that I'll mix the five of you up," Jacqueline admitted.

"There's an easy way to tell us apart. For example, I have one uneven tooth. Look."

She bared her teeth in a forced smile. Then she gave her new friend a physical characteristic unique to each of her sisters, details that Jacqueline tried to memorize.

"Let's go outside," Annette finally suggested. "It's damp in here."

They went out to the playground encircled by the observation gallery.

"When I was little, this seemed enormous."

Jacqueline heard the nostalgia in her friend's voice. She took out the piece of chalk she always kept in her pocket.

"Let's play hopscotch."

"Hopscotch? I don't know how."

Jacqueline drew a hopscotch pattern on the pavement, explaining the rules of the game as she went.

"Watch me do it."

When it was her turn to throw her pebble and jump through the squares, Annette felt light and free — the

98

exultant feeling of being an ordinary girl like any other.

• • •

On their own, the quints avoided forming a group in the refectory, sitting instead at different tables to mix in with their classmates. Since there were only four tables, Émilie and Annette were sitting at the same table, one beside Jacqueline, the other facing her.

The assistant cook came in from the kitchen, pushing a cart with the dishes on it. "You're allowed to talk," she said, noticing the silence in the room. "I know I'd take advantage of that!"

The merry woman's advice fell on deaf ears, for the girls were still too self-conscious to speak. They studied each other furtively and blushed when they were caught in the act. Perhaps it was because there were five celebrities among them, with whom they would be sharing daily life from now on. Few smiles were exchanged, except between girls who, like Jacqueline and Annette, had gotten to know each other. When they did talk, they limited themselves to the necessary banalities: "Could you pass the bread, please?"

The same reserve reigned all evening and continued when they went to the drawing room, where the beds were set out around a grand piano. Then, suddenly, two girls screamed at the top of their lungs: a mouse was running along the keyboard!

"It's the principal's mouse," Annette joked.

They looked at her incredulously. She added, "Be careful what you say, she reports everything back to Sister Aimée-des-Anges."

Even fear of the mouse couldn't keep a few of the girls from laughing. Marie picked up a pillow and chased it

99

away, saying, "Go take a look in the kitchen. I didn't finish my dinner, so there's a nice snack for you."

After a few detours under the beds on which the most fearful girls were crouching, the mouse ran out into the corridor. They heard a frightened shriek, then "Shoo, you filthy rat!" A few seconds later, the night monitor, who slept in a neighboring room, appeared in the doorway.

"Girls, don't make such a fuss over a mouse. Small animals don't eat big ones."

This last sentence, pronounced by a rather plump person whose own fear they had just heard evidence of, made the girls smile, and some exchanged winks.

When the nun had gone back to her room, the girls put on their nightgowns and prepared to go to bed. As they had in the refectory, the quints spontaneously dispersed among the others. But while they were filled with happiness, the other girls seemed rather sad. Funny that these opposing feelings should have the same source: being away from home.

After the mouse incident, Cécile thought it wouldn't take much to break the ice once and for all. She sat up in bed and said, "I have a riddle."

Intrigued, the others looked at her, then gathered round when she beckoned. She glanced over at the door and then whispered, "What's black, white, black, white, black, and then red?"

They looked at each other, trying to find an answer — except for Cécile's sisters, who already knew. In fact, Yvonne was wondering whether her sister's joke was in very good taste.

"You got us," one girl said, finally. "What is it?"

"A nun who falls down the stairs and has a nosebleed."

The laughs bubbled up, and the girls tried to smother

them with their hands. Cécile asked another riddle, and her classmates sat on the two neighboring beds. Then Annette took over, telling joke after joke. Soon, every girl had told a joke or riddle of her own. And by nine-thirty, at lights out, it felt as though they'd known each other forever.

As they lay down, Yvonne and Émilie exchanged happy looks: yes, their dream was coming true beyond all their expectations.

● ● ●

Life at Villa Notre-Dame was a constant joy for the quints. They rediscovered the peace they had once known between these same walls, along with the security of ironclad rules that applied equally to everyone. And this time, they had friends their own age from whom they could learn how things went in a real family. The quints didn't have to tell each other how they felt; their radiant faces confirmed that they were all equally happy.

The days passed according to a set schedule. They got up at six-thirty, washed, attended mass in the chapel of the nuns' residence, and then ate breakfast in an atmosphere of merriment. Classes went from eight-thirty to six in the evening, interrupted by two recesses and a one-and-a-half-hour lunch break. Aside from academic subjects, the nuns taught music, singing, physical education, and home economics. At Oliva's express request, for he still dreamed of a show-business career for his quints, the principal had to teach them to write and perform in skits.

When bad weather kept them inside, the girls gathered in the drawing room, where the quints taught the others to waltz. Although everyone liked everyone else, each girl had one best friend. Yvonne was appreciated for her intelligence and initiative, Cécile for her ability to listen, Annette for her devotion, Émilie for her joviality and gentleness, and Marie for her laugh and her hilarious practical jokes. Simple and sincere, the quints had the gift of making others feel important.

The students washed the dishes and cleaned the dormitory, but these tasks, which took only a half hour a day, seemed like a game to the quintuplets, who were used to working much harder; here, they could continue talking and laughing, and no one ever disparaged their efforts. In just a few days, this new life became the norm.

It was only at morning mass that the quints, Marie in particular, really became aware of their luck. Elzire attended the service conducted by the chaplain in the nuns' chapel. Marie could not help but remember her mother yelling at her, ridiculing her, slapping her. It seemed so long ago, and yet it was only one week behind her. Watching the woman praying so devotedly, Marie found it difficult to believe that she was the same person. And she dreaded Friday, when she and her sisters would have to return to the big house for the weekend. She had begun to hope that their departure had transformed their mother, but Elzire's air of annoyance and disapproval when she saw her quints among the other students convinced her of the contrary. Elzire was polite to their classmates after mass, but Marie could see that she had not let go of her mistrust and suspicion.

It was with a heavy heart that the quintuplets left their new friends on Friday evening to go to their parents' house. (They had gotten permission to have supper at Villa Notre-Dame, since it made their mother's life easier.) Depressed, they trudged up the path to the brick house.

From the perspective of the five days they had just had, what loomed ahead seemed like pure hell.

Elzire had left the dishes for them to wash, and as soon as they had dried them, they were bombarded with questions and asked to describe their week down to the smallest detail. The circumspection that they had developed over the last few years led them to speak in generalities and not reveal their pleasure at being away.

After a bit, Yvonne tried to change the subject. "Have you heard from Rachel, Simone, and Lucie, Mom?"

"Yes," Elzire replied. "Each one wrote us a letter. They have a heart, those girls."

"But we're just across the road," Yvonne said, in self-defense. "We see you every morning at mass. Dad comes to school every day."

Whack! With her wet hand, Elzire hit Yvonne's cheek, catching her off guard.

"Are you talking back to me? Already the bad influence of strangers!"

Yvonne regretted having spoken, not because of the slap but because she feared putting her happiness at Villa Notre-Dame at risk.

Later, their father began his own interrogation. He was especially interested in the behavior of the nuns, the chaplain, and the other girls. Had anyone talked about him, or about the Dionne family? Had they said anything to undermine his parental authority? Did they ask personal questions? To each query, the quints answered no, which made their father happy but did not keep him from warning them again not to trust strangers.

No sleeping in for the quints on Saturday morning! During their brief absence, the house had been neglected, and Elzire had made a cleaning schedule that took them the whole day to accomplish. As usual, Marie and Annette were given the longest chore lists, and the others promised to help when they had finished theirs. Their hearts weren't in it, but they resolutely got to work, hoping to finish before supper. More than the work, it was their mother's frequent inspections that demoralized them. She was never satisfied, always finding an excuse for sharp criticism.

• • •

It was with relief that the quints returned to Villa Notre-Dame on Sunday evening. Although her illness had not manifested itself during the first week at boarding school, on Saturday night Émilie had had an epileptic seizure in her bedroom, after her mother had picked a fight with her for no reason.

Yvonne was as happy as her sisters to be back among their classmates, but she could not forget that it was just a respite. This week, too, would end, and they would have to go back to the big house and put up with their father's looks, looks that she knew were the furthest thing from innocent.

The weeks passed, alternating between calm days at boarding school and weekends that always arrived too quickly. Oliva had gotten it into his head to teach the quints to drive. Although Yvonne, Annette, and Cécile managed to repel his advances and defend themselves against his wandering hands, they worried about Marie and Émilie, who were smaller and more submissive. The first three tried to watch over the others, rushing to the car as soon as their father offered to take Émilie or Marie for a drive.

Their father's behavior made their stays at home even

more difficult, but the quints never discussed it, except indirectly. At least knowing that she wasn't the only one suffering through it helped each one not to feel responsible for it. Nothing could explain how a man could act like that with his own children, and they prayed that he would come to his senses. But their prayers went unanswered: far from mending his ways, Oliva was ever more forward.

Exasperated to have no one to turn to, unable to bear the crushing weight of this secret, Annette decided to confide in the boarding school's chaplain, its guardian of conscience. Father Bélanger was an oblate from Ottawa, like his counterpart, Father Sauvé. Annette appreciated his gentleness and patience very much.

They were walking slowly between the boarding school and the nuns' residence when she brought up the problem. She told herself that Father Bélanger and Father Sauvé could discuss it together — surely they would find a solution. At first the words came with difficulty, but soon they were flowing out, fueled by anger. The priest listened to her confidences with his customary calm.

"It's terrible!" Annette concluded with a heartfelt cry.

His hands behind his back, Father Bélanger shook his head, his eyes fixed on the ground. He said, in a monotone, "It's bad, it's true, but it is not up to you to judge your father."

"But he has no right!"

"Leave it to God to carry the weight of souls."

She sighed deeply and fell silent as they approached the yard where the other pupils were playing.

"Let's walk back the way we came," the priest said.

They walked back up the path. To Annette the brick house got bigger with each step: in one window she could see the silhouette of their mother, spying on them.

How could Elzire not know what her husband was doing?

"I can't take it any more, Father. It's not a life . . ."

"Tut, tut. You are committing the sin of despair."

"Others have done worse!"

"Each of us must deal with his own conscience."

"Couldn't you talk to him?" Annette implored. "Maybe he'd stop."

The priest frowned, uncomfortable. He had been warned to be on his guard with Oliva Dionne, and not to provoke him. He sought a response that would not involve him too deeply and would allow him to save face.

"Even if we are not in the confessional, I must keep your secret. What you tell me, I don't have the right to repeat."

Annette suddenly felt very faint. Their mother was still watching them; next Saturday she would want to know what they had talked about. This depressed her no end.

"What can we do, Father?"

"Continue to respect your father. 'Thou shalt honor thy father and mother . . .' It's a commandment."

Since the girl still didn't seem satisfied, he added, "Pray and have faith in divine providence."

"But the car trips?" Annette insisted, impatiently.

"Wear thick coats."

The bell announced the end of recess. Annette thanked the priest and turned toward the school.

"I'll pray for you," he said.

She ran back to the red building, unhappier than ever, disappointed by the man whom she had considered a friend. *Wear thick coats!*

• • •

The arrival of spring always made Cécile feel euphoric. But this year, when she had just turned fourteen, it was with a certain nostalgia that she watched the leaves unfurling on the aspens and the thickets of pussy willows blooming along the road. Summer was coming, and school would be over for two months. Cécile and her sisters would soon be back in their rooms upstairs in the big house. Their friends from Villa Notre-Dame would go on vacation; her sisters Simone and Lucie would come home. Everything would be just as it was before.

One Saturday evening in May, as she was coming back from the "Mary's month" prayer service, Cécile had a sudden misgiving. She ran into Émilie's room; Émilie had stayed home, since she had just had a seizure. She wasn't there. Cécile looked in the other bedrooms and the bathrooms, then in all the rooms on the ground floor. Émilie was nowhere to be found. Oliva had gone out in the car. Could Émilie be with him? She wasn't well enough for a car ride. Maybe he had taken her to the doctor. No, if she had been sicker, her father would have had Dr. Joyal make a house call.

Cécile's anxiety mounted, but she didn't tell anyone. She hoped so much that she was worrying for nothing. In the basement, perhaps? She went downstairs. Chopin was playing softly on the phonograph in the playroom. There was Émilie sitting on the floor, huddled in a corner.

"Em! What's wrong?"

Her arms hugging her folded legs, Émilie was sobbing. Cécile sat down beside her and stroked her hair.

"Are you sick?"

Her "no" was hoarse and plaintive.

"Is it Mom?"

Cécile quickly realized the absurdity of this question: her mother was in the chapel. A scary thought came to mind.

"Dad?"

At this word, Émilie's sobs intensified. Cécile tapped her own cheek.

"My God!"

With rage in her heart, she drew her sister to her, enclosed her in her arms, and rocked her. Émilie let loose a torrent of sobs from the depths of her body. Cécile cried too, silently, so that her sister would think she was strong.

"Cécile . . ." Émilie cried in a breaking voice.

Cécile patted her back and held her more tightly.

"It's over, Émilie, it's past."

For the first time in her life, she felt hate. She detested this man who claimed to be their father. Why was he always after them? Why not send them away, if he didn't love them? Cécile was ashamed of these thoughts, but she could not get them out of her mind. He had complete power over them, that was the law, and he was the one who took care of them. They could only endure and be patient until they were of legal age. He would have Cécile's respect — or, rather, its appearance, a respectful fear, for she was not ungrateful — but he would not have her love.

After long minutes of crying, Émilie hiccuped, "Don't tell anyone . . ."

"Don't worry."

Cécile meant that she had nothing more to fear from her father, that it wouldn't happen again. Oh, no, he would never touch Émilie again, Cécile promised herself.

Later, after she had reassured her sisters about Émilie's condition, Cécile ordered them, "We must never leave Em all alone when we are here. One of us must keep an eye on her twenty-four hours a day. Understood?"

Marie, Yvonne, and Annette nodded. They understood only too well. Cécile didn't have to say another word.

"Me neither," Marie begged her sisters, "don't leave me all alone."

• • •

When school ended, the eve of Saint-Jean-Baptiste Day, the news fell like a bomb: next September, the quints would be day students at Villa Notre-Dame! This meant that they would sleep and eat at home. No more lively dormitory, no more fun during meals! They would see their friends only during classes and recess. Cécile was now firmly convinced that their father didn't love them, that he was deliberately denying them what would make them happy — and what would be best for them.

When they protested, very weakly, Oliva lectured them again about his mistrust of strangers. And he concluded, in a firm voice, "Morally, those people are taking you farther and farther from your parents. They are there to divide our family once again!"

Elzire agreed and added, "It's like that idea of giving you different names!"

Their mother was not pleased that Sister Aimée-des-Anges had given Annette the nickname "Netta": to get a new name was a little like becoming another person, or leaving the past behind. However, the others also had nicknames invented by a priest, a nun, or a friend: "Cis" for Cécile, "Em" for Émilie, "Peewee" for Marie, because she was the smallest, and "Ivy" for Yvonne. Among themselves, the quints no longer used anything but these nicknames — except when they were at home, because it enraged Elzire.

109

Their parents' decision was final, and the quintuplets had to give in. All hope vanished as the happiness of ten months outside the house evaporated. Then Marie, Yvonne, Annette, and Cécile thought of Émilie.

"She mustn't come back here!" Yvonne declared.

Cécile volunteered to ask Lucie to intervene. She would have to be crafty, but at the same time truly open her heart. When she had an opportunity, she got Lucie outside by inviting her for a walk, though, of course, they couldn't leave the compound. They strolled toward Villa Notre-Dame, stopping in the field to pick violets.

"Have you heard about our boarding school?" Cécile asked.

"Oh, yes!" Lucie exclaimed, seeming truly sorry.

"We're very disappointed."

"I can imagine . . ."

Cécile let a moment of silence pass before saying, "I know that Dad won't change his mind. Not for all five of us, in any case."

"You're right about that."

"Lucie," Cécile pleaded, "Émilie mustn't come back. It makes her sick. She, at least, should go on being a boarder. You could get Dad to allow that, Lucie. Just for one of us. It's extremely important, you must see that."

Cécile was convincing enough that Lucie consented to talk to their father, and he agreed that Émilie would be a boarder for her four remaining years of high school. He and Elzire still harbored an irrational fear of epilepsy, and that made the decision easier.

• • •

On the first day of vacation, Elzire went outside and found the quints sitting on the steps, chatting.

"Don't just sit there — your father doesn't like it! How many times do I have to tell you? Get busy, go on. Go weed the garden." She shooed them off with a wave of her hand. "Not you, Annette, I want to talk to you."

While her sisters went to the vegetable patch, Annette followed her mother to the porch swing, where they sat down facing each other. Elzire wiped her damp forehead with a handkerchief and tucked it back in her skirt pocket.

Abruptly, she asked, "What went on between you and Father Bélanger?"

"Nothing." Annette was caught by surprise.

"Now, don't take me for an idiot!"

"I don't know what you mean, Mom."

"I'm talking about the chaplain," Elzire said dryly. "I saw you together all the time."

Annette defended herself without raising her voice or changing her tone. "He's my guardian of conscience, Mom. That's why we walked together sometimes during recess."

"A guardian of conscience, you say? What keeps that warm at night? Do you love him, is that it?"

"Of course not!" Annette protested strongly.

"What did he do to you?"

"Nothing, I swear. We talked. Anyway, we were always in plain sight."

"But in a hallway, behind a door, eh? It doesn't take much time! Did you kiss through the grille of the confessional?"

"Never in my life!"

"Liar!"

"Nothing happened, I swear."

"Tell me everything. Did he undress you?"

"Mom!" Annette cried as she stood up. The porch swing squeaked as it began to sway.

"Sit down. I'm not finished!"

The relentless interrogation continued. In the end, her mother's insinuations and gratuitous accusations drove Annette to tears. The next day, and the day after that, it started all over again; it went on week after week, until Annette no longer knew if what her mother was suggesting was true or if she had made it up.

On the last day of vacation, Elzire stopped asking the usual questions. She simply said, smiling, "You had a rough summer, didn't you, my girl?"

• • •

For the quintuplets, the happiness of seeing their friends again on the first day of school could not overcome the deep malaise they felt when they saw their father loading Émilie's large suitcase into the trunk of his car. From now on, they would be separated. Émilie would continue to board at Villa Notre-Dame, as they had all done the previous year, while her sisters would eat and sleep at home. Marie, Annette, Yvonne, and Cécile were happy for Émilie, but only in their heads; in their hearts, they felt torn. And Annette realized that she had been completely out of her mind to dream of going far away alone. It was easy to imagine herself alone and cut off from her sisters when she lived with them all the time; it would be completely different when the separation was real!

In spite of the quints' desire for independence, the idea of living apart from one another turned out to be practically intolerable. For as long as they could remember, the perception that each had of the world and of people had been the product of a pooling of their impressions — the

112

sharing of a word, a look, or simply an expression. Each knew that she could count on her four sisters, and each felt responsible for the others. Even though no separation, no matter how long, could ever affect the depth of the love that united them, it would require that they learn a new way to live.

Yvonne made her way to school down the path, which was now barely visible. During elementary school, there had been twelve little Dionnes walking along it at least four times a day, and the sum of all their steps had worn the grass away to the root. Last year, there had been only five going back and forth twice a week, which had allowed the vegetation to take over once again.

Cécile, Émilie, Marie, and Annette also kept their eyes on the ground in front of their feet, and their thoughts differed little from Yvonne's. Annette kicked at a thistle that scratched her ankle. She noted, in a tone that she wanted to sound sarcastic but that came out as great weariness, "Yes, we'll do as the cows do, from the field to the stable, from the stable to the field. We'll make a new trail in the hay."

Émilie wasn't happy to be the only one to escape daily life in the big house, with its fights and chores. She would no longer be able to take up her share of these burdens, and she felt that she was letting her sisters down. Even life in boarding school seemed less wonderful because she would be the only one experiencing it. It would have been so good to have all five sleeping in the same room, among their classmates. And without the presence of her sisters, she was more scared of her illness.

"I would have so loved . . ." she began.

"It would have been impossible for all five of us."

Cécile answered the half-spoken thought. "It was enough that Dad let you be a boarder."

Marie was happy for Émilie. She, too, would have liked to take refuge five days out of seven in boarding school, and the preceding year now seemed like a paradise that she could never get enough of. If she had known . . . Not to give her thoughts away, she said, ironically, "Poor Em, the big house will be missing you!"

Only Émilie smiled. It was not that she found the remark funny, but Marie's effort to make light of the situation moved her.

"Exercise, above all!" Émilie retorted, pretending to wash a floor.

This time, they all burst out laughing.

● ● ●

The four quints who slept in their parents' house every night felt like beasts in a treadmill. In the morning, they joined their classmates for mass, then went back to the house to make breakfast and wash the dishes before rushing to school. At noon, they gobbled their lunch in fifteen minutes, then served the hired help who worked on the family farm and cleaned the dining room and kitchen. When school ended, at six o'clock, the lunchtime routine was repeated. After supper, cleaning the house kept them busy until they went to bed, at nine-thirty.

The months piled up and became years, which resembled each other to the point of melding in memory, as the quints' daily life followed an immutable routine. They never left the compound except with their father. On Saturdays, he sometimes took them and their classmates to a cottage he had bought on the shore of Lake Nipissing. Evenings, he often insisted that they accompany him to the movies in North Bay, with a police escort. The presence of the policemen, who stood at the back of the theater, only made people curious, and it robbed the quints of any pleasure they might have had in the films.

They hated riding in the black Cadillac, which held bad memories for all of them. The one who had the rotten luck to sit beside Oliva had to fend off his wandering hands, for even the presence of the other girls did not dissuade him. His advances continued, and became even more pressing and explicit. Émilie confided to Annette and the chaplain that her father had made her promise to show him her breasts. In the moonlight, he had kissed Cécile passionately and then proposed that she become his mistress. He promised that he would buy her nice clothes in return!

One day, Elzire told Yvonne to go for a ride with her father, who had something to tell her. He drove her to the cottage. As he cut the engine, he said, "Go inside and lie down on the bed. I'll join you in a minute."

"What?!" she couldn't believe her ears.

"Your mother told me that you visit your brothers in their bedrooms at night. If you do it with them, you can do it with me."

"It's not true, Dad! She was lying. She doesn't love me and she wants revenge. I don't go in the boys' rooms!"

She didn't have the courage to say that, on the contrary, it was her brothers who constantly harassed her and her sisters, trying to surprise them when they were getting undressed. Complaining about this to her father would not change anything; it might even excite him more.

· "I swear, Dad," she pleaded. "It's not true. Mom lied!"

He turned toward his daughter, his eyes bright with desire. He stretched his hand toward her chest, and she pressed herself against the car door. In a feverish voice, he said, "You'll like it."

"No!" she cried, struggling out of the car.

She ran to the lake, desperate, terrorized by the idea that he would take her by force. She looked at the birch woods on her left, ready to flee if he was too insistent. A thought had been planted in her, as painful as a splinter deeply imbedded in the palm of her hand: her mother knew everything! Or, at least, she had guessed. And she was doing nothing to help — on the contrary, she had deliberately sent her along with her father, after telling him the made-up story about her sexual adventures.

Would all of this end one day? Yvonne looked at the water so deep it seemed black. If only she weren't responsible for her sisters . . . If only God would save her from all this . . . Then the Cadillac turned in the driveway and an impatient blast from the horn summoned her.

The trip home was silent. Oliva, brooding, stared at the road ahead. Yvonne told herself that her father couldn't love her or he would never have acted this way, that he loved neither her nor her four sisters. They were his property, nothing more.

Their father's behavior made life hell for the quints, but they could do nothing: they were his legal wards and no one would come to help them. The few people who knew refused to get mixed up in it, out of fear of Oliva; the nuns simply told them to pray. The new principal had even added, "This shouldn't keep you from showing him your affection." As for confiding in their friends, the shame was too great. The other girls all had an excellent opinion of Oliva Dionne, whom they saw as a good father. He came to the boarding school each day, in a suit and tie, to bring the mail to the nuns, and stayed to watch the students in their gymnastics class. Only his daughters could imagine what was going on in his head as he watched the young female bodies in motion.

Elzire had stopped hitting the quintuplets, but she continued to be strict and demanding, never satisfied with their efforts. She still chose their clothes and hairstyles: dresses and coats too big and out of fashion, hats more appropriate for elderly ladies, unflattering haircuts. In an effort to draw them closer to her, she told them over and over how unhappy she was and constantly disparaged their father. Though most of their brothers and sisters had either gotten married, like Armand and Rachel, or were away at school, life in the big house was still a constant round of fights, arguments, and tears.

5

"Marie!"

"Jacinthe!"

The two sixteen-year-old girls kissed each other on the cheek, delighted to be reunited after their summer vacation. The other thirteen girls, most of whom had been attending Villa Notre-Dame for four years now, were just as jubilant.

In addition to their happiness, the quintuplets now felt a tremendous sense of deliverance. Summer in the big house had seemed so long! They had avoided talking about it, afraid that the walls themselves had ears, but each knew how the others felt — they were all equally bored and impatient. How many times had Marie caught Yvonne leaning out a window, gazing dreamily at the deserted boarding school!

"You didn't answer my last letter!" Jacinthe reproached Marie gently.

"It was your turn to write me!" retorted Marie.

"I did. I told you about Paul, the boy I met at the ball field."

Marie bit her lower lip and clenched her fists. She had never gotten this letter. Her mother, of course.

From what she knew about the quints' family situation — by observation and deduction, since they never mentioned their parents — Jacinthe could guess what had happened. She took Marie's arm and said, comfortingly, "The letter must have been lost in the mail. It's no big deal. I'll tell you about it now. It's much better this way."

As they drew away from the others for a private chat, Marie looked enviously at Émilie's suitcase at the bottom of the stairs. For three years, Émilie had been boarding at Villa Notre-Dame, coming to the big house only on weekends. Émilie had been spared some of the misery of the summer, Marie thought, but she was as apprehensive as her sisters about the future.

Marie remembered how, when they were just twelve years old, she and her sisters had been confident about their future. *We were so naive,* she thought. Now she couldn't imagine when they would be able to walk freely beyond the walls that imprisoned them. Something would happen, she used to think, an event, a shift in her parents' attitude. But nothing had changed. And, like Émilie, Yvonne, Annette, and Cécile, Marie had resigned herself to an existence of total dependence and unhappiness. The house and the school: it was as if they were leading two parallel lives that bore no relationship to each other.

"Are you listening, Peewee?" Jacinthe asked. They were behind the schoolhouse, walking slowly.

"Of course. Go on." In fact, Marie had not been paying much attention to her friend's story.

"What's bothering you?"

"Oh, nothing," Marie said evasively.

"You know I'm your friend. Whatever you tell me stays between us."

"I know." She held Jacinthe's arm more tightly. They walked a bit in silence before she finally said, "When boarding school ends, we'll lose you."

"I'll always be your friend, Peewee. And anyway, that's a long time from now. Two whole years!"

"But you'll be gone, and the others will, too. What will happen to the five of us?"

Marie didn't dare voice her worst fears. The friends they had made at Villa Notre-Dame were the best thing the quints had ever known: to these friendships they owed all the moments of joy that had been sprinkled through the last three years. And they had no idea what would happen next. It all depended on what their parents decided.

Although they were unhappy, they couldn't conceive of any other life; the real world was a complete mystery. They had no inkling of what awaited them at the end of secondary school, nor even any idea of what to wish for.

Marie finished her thought out loud. "I think I'd like to become a nun."

"Do you feel the vocation? Do you hear the call of the Lord?" Jacinthe asked, very interested.

"I think so, yes."

Marie was stretching the truth a bit. For her and her sisters, religious life sometimes seemed to be the only way out.

As they turned the corner of the building, Jacinthe pointed at the high fence around the yard. "Think about it, Peewee. The convent is another kind of cage. Before you make your decision, get out of here and see a bit of the world, meet people."

120

Jacinthe wanted to sound encouraging, but she wasn't at all sure that she was saying the right thing. Like the quintuplets' other friends, she wondered if they would ever leave the compound. One thing was certain: her famous companions would never have a normal life — not because they didn't want one or weren't capable of it, but because the world wouldn't let them. She had seen for herself the curiosity they aroused — a curiosity that was friendly but nevertheless keen, invasive, and sometimes annoying. Even Jacinthe's own parents were curious. Only to her and the other boarders and the nuns who taught them were the quintuplets girls like any others: Em, Peewee, Ivy, Cis, and Netta. No one else ever used these beloved nicknames.

● ● ●

"Girls! Girls!"

The new principal, Sister Marie-Reine-des-Cœurs, had to yell to make herself heard. When the weather was warm, the nuns and their students often wandered to the woods bordering the field behind Villa Notre-Dame, where the girls sat in twos and threes among the trees and studied.

Thinking they were being called back for classes, the girls dragged their feet as they headed back to the schoolhouse. Cécile, Jacqueline, and Annette were still nowhere to be seen. A nun went out into the field and called the slowpokes, but they were out of earshot, and she had to go and look for them.

Once everyone was gathered around her, the principal slid her hands down the apron she wore over her habit. Her face was glowing and her eyes sparkled behind her steel-rimmed glasses.

"I have great news! Cardinal Spellman, in New York, has invited Ivy, Netta, Cis, Peewee, and Em to attend a banquet to raise funds for needy children."

There were murmurs of excitement, and the other girls turned toward the quintuplets to congratulate them or sigh, "Lucky . . ."

"You've been keeping secrets!" Jacinthe whispered teasingly to Marie.

"Girls! Quiet, please, I'm not finished. Your five friends have asked that you go with them. So, in one month, we'll all be going to New York . . ."

The class erupted in whoops of joy. Most of the girls had never set foot in a large city, and they all began talking at once. Only the quintuplets remained calm, even uncomfortable, exchanging looks of consternation.

"You wanted to surprise me, didn't you?" Jacinthe asked Marie.

Marie shook her head, forcing a smile. She hadn't known herself, and neither had her sisters. Once again, everything had been decided without consulting them.

"You don't look very happy about it, Marie."

"I'm just surprised . . ."

"What do you mean?" Jacinthe asked. "You mean, you . . ."

Marie made a disgusted face. *We're treated like sheep,* she thought, *expected to follow without asking questions.*

"I'm so happy you're all coming with us," Marie declared, concerned that her friends might have misunderstood her reaction. "Otherwise . . ."

The trip itself, with its burden of public appearances, meeting important people, and photo sessions, was hardly an entrancing prospect to the quints. Émilie was worried that she might have an epileptic seizure in pub-

122

lic, and Cécile was scared that her parents might argue in front of her friends.

The principal described a banquet with 2,500 guests, at which the quints were to sing. They were used to performing, since the North Bay radio station recorded them two or three times a year for special broadcasts on Christmas, Easter, and Mother's Day.

"It would be good if you could sing a few songs in English," the principal explained. "Sister Lucille-des-Anges will teach you 'East Side, West Side.' It's a song about New York City. Any questions?"

They all spoke at once. The nun had to call for silence and insist that they ask one question at a time.

"Will we see the Statue of Liberty?"

"I hope so."

"How will we get there, Sister?"

"By train. Mr. Dionne told me that a car has been reserved for us."

Mr. Dionne! Marie fumed. *Even if he wasn't interested in our opinion, he could at least have told us about this trip. We must have looked stupid when Sister Marie-Reine-des-Cœurs made the announcement.*

• • •

Not surprisingly, the quints were not nearly as excited as their classmates. From their experiences at the anniversary celebrations in Ottawa and their brief excursions to North Bay, they knew that during the five days they were in New York they would be constantly scrutinized by crowds of strangers, who would note their every gesture and movement and report back to the newspapers. They would comment on the quints' clothes, hair, the color of their hats — and heaven forbid that one of them should commit the slightest gaffe!

As the date of departure approached, activity became feverish at Villa Notre-Dame, and some classes were cancelled so that they could rehearse the songs they would be performing. A seamstress from North Bay came to take the girls' measurements so that she could make them identical dresses. The nuns had bought high-heeled shoes for the quints, and every day in their bedrooms they practiced walking without tripping. The extra two and a half inches of height thrilled Annette, who had always dreamed of being tall. She was sixteen and should have been growing, but she had not grown at all in two years, and she was not yet resigned to the idea that she would never be more than five feet two inches tall.

A large group accompanied Oliva Dionne when he boarded the train in North Bay that October, 1950. As well as the fifteen students, three nuns, and a nurse for Émilie, there was Mrs. Vézina, who had once taught the quintuplets and had been fired by Dr. Dafoe because he felt she was too close to the Dionne family. Elzire trusted her and had chosen her to take her place because she wasn't up to the trip. Also part of the delegation were Mort Felman, the publisher of the North Bay *Nugget* and an old friend of Oliva's, and several priests. In Ottawa, the city's bishop, Monseigneur Vachon, and Father Sauvé joined the group.

After the train crossed the border into the United States, the quintuplets' nerves began to get the better of them. Although they knew their songs to perfection, they didn't feel prepared for what was ahead. To whom would they be introduced? What would they have to do and say? Émilie reminded her sisters of the magical time when

124

they were children and nothing could upset or intimidate them.

"I can't believe that was really me," Marie sighed.

And Jacinthe had thought Marie would be comfortable appearing in public! Jacinthe had been planning to watch her for clues on how to act and which utensil to use with each dish! But it was Marie who really needed a helping hand.

"We'll get through it," Yvonne said confidently.

"Who knows?" Cécile added. "It might even be fun."

Annette didn't join the conversation. She was haunted by something Father Sauvé had said an hour before: "Did you know that your father wanted to sell you girls to a circus when you were born?"

"Oh, yes," she had answered in a voice she hoped sounded casual, as if she had known this astonishing fact for a long time. She didn't want to hear more painful details. Their father had wanted to sell them . . . So, it wasn't surprising that he respected them so little.

Annette felt as though she had known the story her whole life. It was one of those things that one knew but pushed to a dark corner of one's mind and avoided thinking about. There were so many secrets hidden away within her. No one had ever told her her own story; she had learned bits and pieces and figured out the rest from a word caught on the fly, an allusion decoded, the end of a sentence hanging in the air when she entered a room, a revealing passage in a newspaper or magazine article describing their childhood for the thousandth time. The story that hadn't been told was about hate and money, and its dominant themes were guilt, shame, and resentment.

"What do *you* think, Netta?"

Annette started, and Émilie put her question another way. "Cis thinks the trip could be like a vacation."

"That would be wonderful!" Annette answered.

But the stay in New York turned out to be more like a race against the clock. Everything was planned and organized down to the last detail, and no free time was allotted. Reporters, flashbulbs, and microphones were everywhere. People gathered wherever the quintuplets appeared with their "retinue," and everywhere they went, policemen came along to protect them from the fervor of their fans. And then there were the interminable official ceremonies: dinner with Cardinal Spellman, mass at St. Patrick's Cathedral, where they were seated in the chancel, and the annual Alfred E. Smith banquet, costing $100 per person, where the quints were introduced to the vice-president of the United States and innumerable prelates, ambassadors, and businessmen. Each time, after the customary greetings were exchanged, they fell silent, not knowing what to say to people they didn't know. The longer they had to stand and pose with the celebrities for the photographers, the more withdrawn they became.

None of their classmates was the least bit envious of their fame. On the contrary, they knew how much these social events bothered the quints, how much the constant presence of the cameras and insistent stares exhausted them. Although they admired how easy the quints made it look to stand up in front of a crowd, they remembered a remark that Lucie Dionne had once made to a reporter: "I wouldn't be in their shoes for anything in the world!"

When it was finally time to leave for home, a large crowd gathered on the platform of Grand Central Station to see them off. Taken by surprise, they signed the autograph books thrust at them and waved back at their

126

admirers. This displeased Oliva Dionne greatly. As the train began to roll, he took them aside to scold them soundly: *No autographs! No conversations! No waving!*

"Have a shred of dignity," he told them. "Know your place. No familiarities."

But he sells his own autograph! Marie thought rebelliously, though, like Annette, she had no idea where this knowledge came from. It was obvious that her father was jealous. He showed the quints off proudly enough, but as soon as they were getting the lion's share of the attention, he got upset. Without listening to what he was saying, she watched her father as he lectured them. What she felt for him she either could not or did not want to name.

When the train stopped in Montreal, where the quints were to say a rosary on the radio with Monseigneur Léger, Windsor Station was besieged. The crowd overflowed the barriers erected by the police, and railroad-company employees whisked the quints and their group away to the baggage room. The fans found out where they were hiding and rushed over to press their faces against the large windows, waving their hands and shouting greetings. This time, the quints did not return the waves or react in any way. Their companions, who had found all the attention frightening at first, now saw the funny side of their friends' celebrity.

What happened at Windsor Station upset Oliva, and he kept up his harangue all the way back to Corbeil. When he began again after they got home, Marie finally retorted, "It's not our fault if people want to see us!"

"All you have to do is pretend you don't see them!" Oliva thundered.

"We didn't ask to go to New York."

"That's enough! I've had enough of your lip! Don't talk

back to your father. On your knees in the corner until dinner."

Marie obeyed with no further protest, since her father's voice was trembling with barely restrained rage. *It's so unfair,* she thought as she stared at the wall. *He treats me like a child, even though I'm sixteen years old. He thinks he can keep me from growing up and becoming a woman.*

• • •

The high heels were put away in a cupboard and the quints slipped back into their Villa Notre-Dame boarding-school uniforms, happy for the sense of anonymity they provided. Time was rushing too quickly toward a moment they dreaded: the end of high school. The year following the trip to New York blended in with the three previous ones so seamlessly that they wouldn't have noticed it passing except for the depression and distress in their hearts. Then came an event that, if Annette's imagination hadn't taken flight, would no doubt have been nothing more than another chore. They were to be introduced to Princess Elizabeth and the Duke of Edinburgh, who were making a stopover in North Bay on their visit to Canada.

"I'll ask her to help us," Annette told her sisters.

"You're crazy!" Yvonne exclaimed. "She'll laugh at you, or pretend she didn't hear you."

"Maybe not. After all, we're wards of the King. And remember, the Queen gave us a kiss once!"

"We gave her a kiss," Yvonne corrected her.

"That's true. But being wards of the King must mean something, all the same! The Princess will have no choice but to listen to us."

No one contradicted her. Émilie, Marie, Cécile, and Yvonne were beginning to find Annette's idea intriguing. The expression "ward of the King" had always been magical for them, for they had believed since childhood that it meant they were somehow related to the royal family.

"We met the Princess's mother. Perhaps we should ask how she is," Émilie suggested.

"Let's not get carried away," Cécile said, waving her hand for calm.

"Don't you think we should tell the Princess about our situation?" Annette asked her.

"I didn't say not to, but I'm not going to be the one who does it!"

Everyone turned and looked at Yvonne. She shook her head firmly. "Me neither."

Annette sighed. "All right. I'll do it. We'll write a letter and I'll give it to her."

"She might not read a letter," Marie objected. "But if we talk to her, she'll have to listen to us."

"That's true," Annette conceded. "I'll talk to her." She looked at each of her sisters in turn, then continued: "If anyone else is interested . . ."

There were no volunteers. "Does she speak French?" she asked anxiously.

"Be prepared to speak in either language," Cécile suggested.

A few days later, Oliva and Elzire drove the quintuplets to the North Bay airport. Squeezed between her sisters on the back seat, Émilie thought again about the trip to Toronto that they had made when they were six to see the King and Queen of England. She remembered it well, and when she looked at the press clippings in her father's collection, she could put names to the images engraved on her memory. "Quintland Express" had been written in large golden letters on bright-red train cars, specially prepared and decorated to mark the quints' first trip away from their hospital.

What had particularly impressed the quintuplets were the roomettes in which they slept — it was the first time they hadn't all slept in the same room! The nurses and the teacher had slept in their car; another car had been for their parents, brothers, and sisters; yet another one carried Dr. Dafoe and the members of their guardianship council; and a last one was for the fifty reporters and photographers who were coming along on the trip.

Everywhere the train slowed down, people were gathered along the tracks to wave to them. In Toronto, it was worse: people were standing ten deep on either side of the street, and police motorcycles had to clear a path. Standing on the back seat of a big convertible, the quints calmly contemplated the streams of smiling faces and waving hands, some of them brandishing little red flags with blue lines. Spontaneously, the little girls began to blow kisses to the enchanted crowd. No one had told them to do this; they had simply wanted to make people happy.

It had been the same thing all the way to the Ontario parliament buildings at Queen's Park. After running a gauntlet of photographers with their flashbulbs popping, the quints found themselves in a waiting room, where they changed into long white flounced organdy dresses and matching bonnets. Then they were shown into a stateroom, where they joined Dr. Dafoe, their father and mother, their three brothers in dark blue suits, and their three sisters in dresses and bonnets of white crepe very similar to theirs.

It was then that an usher told Elzire that only the quints and their parents would have an audience, not the other children. She was furious! After all, the invitation had been addressed to Oliva and his "family." The employee in his fancy uniform knew nothing about this, nor did he want to. In Elzire's eyes, it was a cruel injustice. The children had been so excited about meeting the King and Queen; to be rejected like this, as they were about to enter the room, was mortifying.

King George VI was very impressive in his navy officer's uniform. As for Queen Elizabeth, she smiled kindly when Émilie and her sisters curtseyed in perfect unison. The quints waited for the monarch to ask their names, as had been planned, so that they could reveal their identities according to a protocol they had learned by heart. But nothing happened. The Queen just looked at them, smiling. Cécile told herself that they would have to improvise. She said to her sisters, "A kiss for the Queen."

She stepped forward, her arms spread, toward the woman, who, after a moment's hesitation, leaned down to let the child kiss her. One after another, the quints put their arms around the Queen's neck and planted noisy kisses on her cheeks.

"They're charming!" Queen Elizabeth said to Elzire.

"Marvelous, marvelous," the King said.

"Where are the princesses?" Annette asked. "Why didn't you bring them?"

Charmed by their spontaneity, the Queen answered, "They would have liked to come, but we thought that would make the trip much more complicated."

Then she gave the quints small white coats as gifts, and they gave her photographs of them on which they had written dedications to the princesses. Everyone then followed the King and Queen across the floor of the Legislature, parading past the politicians and looking up

131

at the guests crammed into the balcony. Émilie blew a kiss, and the crowd, which had been silent, burst into applause.

Émilie couldn't help sighing as the Cadillac stopped near a sign saying, "North Bay, elevation 1,213 feet." How she missed the sense of freedom she had had back when she hadn't known what fear was.

"Will you be all right?" whispered Annette, her face pale with trepidation.

Émilie nodded. In fact, she wasn't thrilled with the idea of telling the Princess their problems.

They joined the group of dignitaries lined up in front of a hangar, and they waited. Annette stared at the ground and studied the tiny cracks that formed a pattern on the asphalt. Around them was a desolate landscape; the ceremony would be nothing like the one marking the visit of the Princess's parents.

A roar of engines announced the arrival of the royal airplane, which landed and taxied to a spot right in front of the guests. A red carpet was unrolled and the young royal couple emerged.

Annette's nervousness was making her throat dry. Would the words come out? Unbeknownst to her, her mother had been in a similar position twelve years before. Elzire had had tucked in her handbag a petition to the Queen asking that her children be given back to her. She hadn't dared to hand the letter over. Annette fiddled with the envelope that contained the photograph of her and her sisters that she had been told to give to the Princess, even though she thought this gift completely inappropriate.

"Stop that. You'll crush it," Elzire muttered to her. "And stop wiggling. You look like you have worms."

Princess Elizabeth emerged from the airplane, dignified in a magnificent mink coat. She didn't seem at all impressed by the welcoming committee. To the quints, she simply said "Hello" and then moved on, her face blank. Annette suddenly realized that, although they were wards of the King, the Dionne quints simply did not exist for the English Princess. Asking for her help had been a crazy, childish idea. Annette kept silent as she shook the gloved hand.

The Duke of Edinburgh was more charming, talking to the quints in both French and English, asking about their school and their plans for the future. He had very bright blue eyes.

Once the couple had climbed into a red convertible and left for a brief tour of the town, the quintuplets stood aside while their parents chatted with acquaintances. None of her sisters reproached Annette for not saying anything. They all felt that they had lost one final illusion. Nothing would ever change: they would always belong to their parents.

"Did you see how rudely she looked at us?" Émilie asked in a low voice.

To hide her disappointment, Annette tried to turn the whole thing into a joke. "Maybe she was trying to say, 'Don't kiss my husband — he belongs to me!'"

Marie concluded, "Anyway, her taste in hats is no better than Mom's . . ."

The joke fell flat; no one had the heart to laugh.

• • •

"Eighteen years old," Elzire Dionne muttered incredulously. "And Dr. Dafoe gave you twenty-four hours to live! Huh! That man . . ."

She dropped a peeled potato into a pot half filled with water. She looked at Cécile, who was sitting on the other side of the kitchen table, then at the pile of peelings accumulating in front of her daughter.

"Too thick," she said. "You're wasting food. Just the skin." Returning to her cooking, she picked up her train of thought where she had left off. "It was St. Theresa and the Holy Virgin who kept you alive. And the good Lord, too, of course. Not Dafoe and those nurses! Prayer makes miracles, never forget that."

No doubt, Cécile thought, *but it doesn't always work.* How many times had she implored God to improve the quints' lot? "God sends you trials to strengthen your souls," her father confessor had replied when she had asked his advice, secretly hoping that he would talk to her parents. "God's designs are unfathomable," the nuns would say to comfort them. "Abandon yourself to His will."

She couldn't be angry at them for not intervening; life would have been unbearable without the priests and nuns.

Elzire, who was deeply religious, continued vaunting the merits of prayer. For her part, Cécile believed in God, but she found that religious education was too big a part of the high school curriculum. Morning mass and prayers at meals and bedtime were fine. But they spent too much time on the superficial parts of religion — for example, the scrapbooks in which, every Friday afternoon, they had to arrange holy images to make clever collages on a specific theme. She had filled up dozens of scrapbooks over the past five years.

None of what they were doing in school — songs, skits, embroidery, and other such things — was preparing them for a career, and school was almost over. For instance, Cécile hadn't taken a single chemistry class, which she would need for nursing school. Never mind, she would catch up — provided her parents gave their permission . . .

"Villa Notre-Dame will be closing," she said to her mother, trying to make it sound like an offhand comment.

"Uh-huh."

"And the five of us . . ."

Since her mother was not picking up her hints, Cécile decided to tackle the subject straight on. She blurted out, "I want to be a nurse."

"A nurse?" Elzire bellowed. "Get that idea out of your head. That's not a profession, wiping people's backsides!"

Cécile pleaded her cause. "Taking care of people is noble."

"I don't want to hear any more about it!"

"We want to continue our education after high school, and prepare for a profession."

Elzire shrugged. "You ask your father what his plans are for you."

"Did he tell you?" Cécile asked, both curious and uneasy.

"You ask him. All right, we have enough potatoes. Go rinse them off."

Cécile did as she was told. It was useless to keep trying; her mother would tell her nothing. Indeed, she might not know anything herself, for Oliva Dionne was not in the habit of consulting her. He simply announced his decisions.

As the end of the school year approached, the quints became more and more obsessed with the question of their immediate future. Finally, Yvonne ventured to ask her father about the following autumn. She reported his answer back to her four sisters, waiting impatiently in the basement playroom.

"He said, 'I know what is best for you. Just study for your final exams.'"

"That's all?" asked Émilie, disappointed.

"That's all." Yvonne sat down heavily on the piano bench, depressed.

"It's not fair!" Cécile exclaimed. "It concerns us! It's our life, after all!"

"I know it bothers you, Cis," Annette said quietly. "You've already decided what you want to do. But I haven't, and if Dad asked me where I wanted to go next fall, I wouldn't know what to answer. I have no idea."

"There are all sorts of professions," Marie murmured mysteriously. For some time, she had been more withdrawn and meditative.

"What do you mean?" Annette asked. "What do you have in mind?"

"The calling of faith . . ."

Her sisters couldn't hide their astonishment. Since Marie didn't go on, Émilie asked her, softly, "Are you serious?"

"I think about it a lot. I pray to see my way more clearly."

The others didn't press the matter. They had all considered, at one time or another, entering a convent, motivated as much by the desire to get out of the house as by faith. But that Marie was still thinking about it surprised her sisters. This notion would pass, they were convinced, once she had tasted a bit of "real" life and met a few new people. Right now, it was useless to argue.

After a brief silence, Yvonne said, "We'll all pray for you, Peewee."

136

"We should pray a little for ourselves, too," Annette added, caustically. "What if Dad decides to keep us home, as servants?"

"He doesn't have the right!" Marie protested.

"He's our father," Annette retorted. "The law is on his side."

"And he's the one who pays," Émilie added. "We couldn't earn a living."

"We've never crossed the street by ourselves," Yvonne joked sadly. "We wouldn't even know how to buy stockings or take a bus."

"We'd learn!" Annette said.

Cécile checked to make sure no one was coming, then she said, firmly, "Right now, it's true, we wouldn't know how to get by in the world. Aside from cleaning house and praying, we don't know much. That's why it's important to learn a profession. Otherwise, we'll never be on our own. We'll always be dependent on Dad and Mom."

"A profession . . . that's easy to say!" Émilie said, and Annette and Yvonne nodded in agreement.

"Yes, a profession, a trade," Cécile replied. "Something to earn a living with! For the first time in our life, we'll have an opportunity to choose something we like, to make our own decisions."

"I hope we can learn how to do that, too," Émilie sighed.

For a moment they all reflected: Marie and Cécile weighed their choices again, while the others wondered what they would like to do. Annette enjoyed music and was a good pianist, but she couldn't see herself playing an instrument her whole life. Teaching music, perhaps . . . Yvonne also wanted to be a nurse, but her desire wasn't as strong as Cécile's and she had not yet dared to make it known to her parents. As for Émilie, none of her wishes seemed as strong as the others'; she knew that she would like to help people, but how?

Finally, Annette returned to the topic that was making them all so uneasy. "And what if Dad wants to keep us at home? What do we do, jump the fence?"

Cécile, the only one who knew about her sister's old dreams of escape, had to smile.

"He wouldn't do that," Émilie said. "Obviously we get on their nerves. They'll want to send us somewhere else."

"From your mouth to God's ear!" Annette cried. "Far away, I hope."

"Especially if he were scared that it would come out in the papers," Marie added. "'The imprisoned quints!'"

Yvonne quieted her sisters with a gesture. "It's been almost nine years since we moved here," she said calmly, "and the worst is past. No matter what, we'll be twenty-one in three years."

"I don't want to turn twenty-one with nothing to show for it," Cécile declared. "Why lose three more years?"

"You're right," Yvonne said, "but let's not get worried before we have to."

"Have you had a lot of pleasant surprises?" Cécile retorted.

"We could always find husbands," said Émilie with a little smile. "The newspapers say now that we're eighteen we can marry without our parents' consent."

"Cis might like that," Annette quipped.

They all burst out laughing, except Cécile. She didn't like it when they needled her about the American boy who had seemed quite taken with her at the winter carnival in St. Paul, Minnesota, several months ago. They had been invited by Brown & Bigelow, a company that

138

had been putting out a calendar featuring a picture of them every year since they were two, and they were the main attraction. For their official appearances, each had been escorted by a "faithful admirer." Cécile's had seemed very attentive, even though he was quite shy. It was the first time they had held hands with boys! They hadn't had a second alone with their escorts, and Oliva had not allowed them to attend the closing ball, but this hadn't kept Cécile from dreaming for weeks afterward of a certain handsome young man.

"What was his name, again?" Marie teased.

Cécile wanted to be annoyed, but her bond with her sisters was too strong, and she laughed too.

● ● ●

Cécile's impatience grew until it was unbearable. One day, when she found her parents alone in the dining room, she asked to have a word with them. Elzire looked at her husband, her knitting needles flashing as fast as ever.

Oliva put his newspaper down on the table and sat up in his chair. "Yes?"

"I want to be a nurse," Cécile blurted out, getting straight to the point to cover her stage fright.

"That's no way to ask," her mother said. "Go sit on your father's lap to ask him."

Cécile shuddered with revulsion. Elzire jerked her head toward Oliva. Cécile's desire to become a nurse was so great that she went and sat gingerly on her father's lap.

Oliva seemed touched by her gesture, and he answered her request softly. "You are young and inexperienced. I would like you to stay with the Sisters of the Assumption for two more years. There's no rush. There's lots of time to decide your future. I've enrolled all five of you in the Family Institute in Nicolet."

Cécile hid her disappointment carefully, having learned long ago how to take bad news with a strong heart.

"Where is Nicolet, Dad?"

"Between Montreal and Quebec City, on the south shore of the St. Lawrence River."

Quebec, a whole province away! As far away as any of them could have hoped. If she insisted now on going to nursing school, it might make Oliva angry, and she didn't want to compromise the chance that was being offered to them. It was half a victory: they would finally escape their parents' grasp, their cloistered life, the barbed-wire fences — and, above all, the looks their father gave them, which made them feel ashamed of their bodies. No more fear of finding themselves alone with him. Freedom!

"Thanks, Mom and Dad, for letting us go away to school," Cécile said, standing up. "You won't be ashamed of us."

"I'm counting on that," Oliva answered.

The news made the other quints happier than it made Cécile. They tried to imagine what their new life would be like, but too much information was missing. What would it mean to be able to go wherever you wanted without asking permission? To be someplace where the horizon wasn't limited by fences that were supposed to protect them? How would they deal with situations they had never encountered before — buying stockings in a store, talking to strangers in the street, taking a bus? There were a thousand little things that were second nature to girls raised "outside" that the quints knew nothing about.

Perhaps because of their sadness at the idea of being separated from their classmates, their first and only

140

friends, the freedom promised for September soon made the quints anxious. They had been told so often not to trust anyone who wasn't part of their small, barricaded world that they were scared of the unknown future awaiting them. Crowds, especially, terrified them. There would no longer be policemen to keep people away, or organizers to tell them what to do. True, people seemed nice, but they could be overwhelming. The autographs, the questions, and especially the curiosity made the quints feel like strange bugs under a microscope.

These apprehensions grew when the quints shared them. They invented ways, each more far-fetched than the last, to protect their privacy, such as taking assumed names, or never traveling as a group of five together, only in twos or threes. Cécile and Annette decided to dye their hair dark brown to avoid being recognized. One evening, they shut themselves in the bathroom with a bottle of hair dye. Although they followed the instructions meticulously, they stained their hands but didn't manage to change their hair color.

• • •

At Oliva's request, the nuns organized an official ceremony for the quints' high-school graduation. In May, decorators built a stage in the playroom in the basement of the Dionne house and nuns came from Sturgeon Falls to orchestrate the ceremony and rehearse the students.

As he did for every special occasion, Mr. Sasse came up from New York to take press photos. The quints posed for three days, first for pictures for a new calendar, and then with the white robes and matching mortarboards that they would wear when they received their high school diplomas.

The ceremony took place with great pomp on May 28, the quints' birthday, attended by a large number of guests. All the Dionne children were there, as were the parents of the other students, a gaggle of clergy, and numerous reporters.

In the room off the playroom, the quints and their nine classmates checked their gowns and awaited the signal to file onto the stage. There was no laughing or joking, just whispering. The girls' serious expressions were due not to the ceremony itself but to their feeling that this was the last time they would all be together. Each would take a different path, and perhaps they would never see each other again, in spite of the friendships that had grown so close over the last five years. Together, they had gone from childhood to adulthood. They promised to write each other and never to forget their high school years.

"We were lucky to go to school with you," Jacqueline whispered in Annette's ear.

"We were the ones who were lucky. You made this the best time of our lives. Without you, I don't know what we would have done."

Although Annette was whispering, everyone heard what she'd said. They furtively wiped their eyes, squeezed each other's hands, hugged and exchanged kisses on the cheek, and vowed eternal friendship. At this moment, the principal opened the door. Moved by this scene, she stayed outside the room for a moment before coughing softly to announce her presence.

"You are all remarkable girls," she said softly. "We are sad to see you go, but at the same time we're very proud. We know that you will be good Christians and that each of you will follow courageously the road that God has chosen for you."

She looked affectionately at the faces flushed with emotion. Then she said, briskly, "And now, girls, let's go. Your guests are waiting for you."

After the ceremony, as they posed with Elzire and Oliva for Mr. Sasse, holding big bouquets of flowers, the quints' smiles were not forced, as they had so often been for the photographer. An era was ending, and a new life was awaiting them — a life that could only be wonderful compared to the one they had endured up to now.

I'm truly proud of my little girls. The girls waited in vain for these words from their father or mother. It would have been a good time to pay them a first compliment. Cécile saw how proud her friends' parents were; her own parents smiled only for as long as it took to take a photograph.

Make believe, she thought.

6

Narrow fields, separated by rectangles of fencing and dotted with giant elm trees, slipped by on either side of the road. Her forehead leaning against the glass of the car window, Annette was amazed at the luxuriance of the countryside. Compared to the harsh, wild landscape of Northern Ontario, the St. Lawrence Valley seemed gentler and more civilized. Perhaps it was symbolic of the change in direction that her life was finally taking. She turned to look at Yvonne, who raised her eyebrows to let her know she was sharing her thoughts.

It had been a long trip from Ontario. Oliva and his eldest son, Armand, had said almost nothing the entire way. *We are strangers to each other,* Cécile thought bitterly. Nine years had passed since the quintuplets had been reunited with their family, and Cécile felt guilty that she had never managed to fulfill her duty to love them. Distance, she hoped, would ease this unpleasant, though unjustified, feeling.

For Marie, each minute seemed to last an hour. She

couldn't wait to see Émilie, who had left for the Institute in Nicolet by train fourteen days ago, accompanied by a nun. Because of her state of health, it had been considered better to let her settle in and get used to the new school before the other boarders arrived. Anyway, there wouldn't have been enough room for all of them in Oliva's Cadillac. Fourteen days was an eternity when you'd never been separated more than one night, and when you loved your sister as much as, if not more than, yourself.

"We're almost there," Cécile whispered to Marie, squeezing her hand.

They had all missed Émilie. She had been gone so long that there had even been time to write her and get a reply. The four quints tried to imagine what the Institute might be like, cobbling together an image from memories of the convents they had stayed at in New York and Ottawa. But it wasn't hard to imagine the welcome that Émilie would have for them. Marie sighed wearily as she noticed that evening was falling.

When the lights of Nicolet appeared, it was almost nine o'clock. Oliva had deliberately chosen to arrive at night. With the streets almost deserted and the Institute's other students in bed, the quintuplets' arrival wouldn't attract attention. Above all, he did not want reporters to be waiting in front of the school. Émilie's early departure had already caused speculation in the press. Oliva liked to meet reporters on his own turf, and only when it suited him.

He had mixed feelings about letting his little girls go. The press would have made a fuss if he had kept them at home and refused them a higher education. The boarding school was a lesser evil; they would not be too

145

much at the mercy of strangers or exposed to unwelcome influences. The nuns would keep an attentive eye on them; he had given strict instructions to this effect. When the other parents came to see their daughters on Sundays, the quints had to be locked up in a classroom so no one would see them — for their own protection, of course. Nor were they allowed visitors other than their parents.

It was completely dark as they drove through Nicolet. Annette was disappointed that she couldn't see the surrounding countryside and the river, but the tree-lined streets and shops enchanted her. She saw herself walking on the sidewalk, alone, and drawing looks, not because she was a Dionne quintuplet but because she was tall and strong. In her daydream, five-foot-two Annette was at least five foot eight, or even five foot ten!

Although they knew that their father would be annoyed, the quints ran toward Émilie when they saw her coming down a corridor. They hugged, exchanging platitudes as their father approached. But it didn't matter; there was no need for words. Their eyes said everything. What dominated this silent conversation was Émilie's pride at having survived all by herself for two weeks and her wish never to undergo such a test again.

Marie was very quiet. She seemed withdrawn, and yet no one was more caught up in this reunion than she. It seemed like the most wonderful moment in her life. No joy had ever been so deep, so intense, as the happiness of being once again with her beloved sister. She realized with astonishment, mixed with fear, that she had not truly lived during the last fortnight. Émilie's absence had been like a gaping hole inside her. She had simply been going through the motions, and all she'd been able to think about was seeing Émilie again. As the blessed day had

146

approached, time had seemed to stand still. Now, Marie felt complete once again.

Once their trunks had been taken down to the basement, where the boarders' lockers were, Émilie took her sisters to the dormitory. She was pleased for once to be the one showing the others the way; for several days, they would count on her, for she had gotten to know the place well.

"Our dormitory is blue and green," she murmured as they walked down the deserted corridors, where the slightest noise seemed to echo loudly. "There are twenty-five of us."

"Twenty-five . . ." Cécile muttered.

There had been fifteen girls at Villa Notre-Dame. Their world was getting bigger. The image of concentric ripples when a pebble broke the surface of a pond came into Cécile's mind. The central point was her parents' large brick house, from which she hoped, over time, to distance herself more and more.

The beds, laid out in five rows of five, were surrounded by curtains for privacy. At five of the beds, the curtains were open. Émilie pointed out her own bed, and her sisters each chose one. They put on their nightgowns and went to the bathroom adjoining the dormitory. There, Annette was unpleasantly surprised to find that the mirrors attached to the wall were too high for her; she would have to stand on tiptoe to see herself. Instead, she used her hand mirror to brush her hair.

"The ones in the locker room are lower," Émilie told her, smiling.

"Do you think I'm going to go down to the basement to brush my hair?" Annette griped.

"I think you're tall," said little Marie, and they laughed.

As Cécile was about to close the curtain around her bed, the curtains of the neighboring bed opened to reveal a girl's friendly face.

"Hi! My name's Rita."

Cécile extended her hand and introduced herself, adding, "They call me Cis."

They exchanged a few hushed words. Rita was both tactful and a natural talker; nevertheless, Cécile discerned in her neighbor a poorly concealed curiosity. She didn't take offense; the newspapers mentioned the Dionne quintuplets almost every week, so it was understandable that people were interested. Cécile had decided before she arrived to give people a chance to ask questions for a few days, so that they could satisfy their curiosity and get to know who the quints really were. Only then would she decide whom she wanted to get to know better.

"Good night, Rita."

"Good night, Cécile."

Although she was tired from the trip, Yvonne couldn't get to sleep. The glow of the dormitory night-light transformed the folds of the curtain into alternating dark and light stripes that looked like prison bars. To reassure herself that they weren't really there, she held her hand out and lightly tapped the fabric. Fences were a thing of the past, as was the heavy step of their father in the hallway. Yvonne felt lighter than ever before, relieved of her life-long responsibility to protect her sisters. Here, there was no danger. God! She had come to doubt that this moment would ever come. How had they gotten through those nine long years?

Today, those years seemed folded in on themselves, a compact, monolithic block, but she knew better. Each year had been an infinity of days, filled with pain, anguish,

148

disappointment, disillusion, and constant despair. There were so few happy memories! Starting today, she could drop her defenses. The feeling of liberty was so exhilarating that she didn't want to go to sleep right away. She wanted to stay awake and drink deeply of it.

Annette couldn't get to sleep, either. Her dreams of escape had finally come true — differently than she had imagined, but true all the same. It was hard for her to believe, and she still worried that something terrible would ruin her happiness. It would be days and days, she knew, before she no longer feared that she would wake up from this beautiful dream. Perhaps she would breathe a little easier when her father left for home. She sat up, parted her curtain a little, and looked around the dormitory to convince herself that this was all real. She could see Marie's bare feet sticking out from under her curtain; kneeling beside her bed, she was praying. Annette lay back down and silently recited a prayer along with her sister.

Marie was saying a prayer of thanks to God for having brought them to Nicolet, and she asked Him to light the way that she should follow now. So many avenues were opening up to her. Everything seemed possible — both the best and the worst. Far from the fences, far from her parents, religious life seemed less attractive. Her doubt had grown stronger with every mile she traveled away from Corbeil.

Suddenly, her curtain opened and Émilie slid into her compartment to kneel beside her.

"Don't worry if you feel a little lost, Peewee. It won't last long. You'll see, we'll be happy here."

"I don't feel lost," Marie replied, her voice barely audible. "I thought I would be, but it's funny, Em, I feel quite

149

at home here. Maybe it's because you were waiting for us."

"Everything is peace here, holy peace."

The allusion was clear for Marie. She squeezed her sister's hand. "I was just thanking the good Lord."

"I'll pray with you for a bit," Émilie said.

And in the dormitory, as their twenty-three classmates breathed peacefully, the two young women thanked Heaven for the happiness they'd found.

• • •

The next day, their father paid the quints a last visit before leaving for Corbeil. His final instructions repeated his usual themes: *Don't trust strangers. Don't talk to strangers. Don't be influenced by classmates or the nuns. Be discreet. Don't answer any questions concerning the family. Above all, never speak to reporters or let yourselves be photographed.*

"Don't make me ashamed of you," he told the girls as they took turns kissing him on the cheek. "Write home every week."

This simulated tenderness repelled Annette, but, like her sisters, she was powerless before her father's authority. If he needed a show of love, they must give it. And she understood well the unstated demand behind his words: the quints should miss their parents and let them know it.

Only after the Cadillac had left the Institute's parking lot did the quints relax. Right up to the last minute, their father could have changed his mind and taken them back home with him. Now, they were finally alone, young women among other young women, and they could begin to find out about their new life.

150

The next three days were devoted to a closed retreat, and then classes began. Cécile soon realized with chagrin that she and her sisters were not taking the same courses as all the others. It was as though the nuns didn't really know what to do with them. Was it because they had been registered at the last minute? Whatever the reason, it bothered Cécile that she was not taking math, a subject in which she was weak and that would no doubt be useful to her later on. At least she was taking the chemistry course she needed to register for nursing school. All the other subjects seemed useless: drawing, knitting, weaving, cooking, embroidering, petit point, singing, music, and arts and crafts — nothing that would prepare the quints for a real profession.

Cécile's daily reports in her diary were laconic. For September 15, 16, and 17, she repeated the same words: "Weaving, knitting." The following day, "Weaving all day." A week of decorative arts began on the 29th, which she summarized as "Drawing, drawing, drawing all day long."

To these subjects were added diction and typing. The quints also rehearsed their singing, for, while the other boarders were studying, they had to perform for a clergyman's visit, a nun's birthday, or at funeral services or masses for the memory of a departed. Often, they were absent from classes three or four days in a row because of this.

"This gets us nowhere!" Cécile complained to Annette.

"But it's fun!"

"I'm not saying it's not, but I still feel like I'm wasting my time."

Cécile said no more; she saw that she was making Annette sad. There was no point in telling her sister about her sense of foreboding, her fear that their father had an ulterior motive for choosing classes that taught them only to be "good little housewives." He no doubt wanted them to come back home to take care of their parents!

Annette searched for something to say to agree with her sister. "It's true that weaving is hard on the back." But she couldn't keep herself from adding, "But less than washing seven bathroom floors down on all fours!"

Cécile smiled. No doubt, she was too impatient and didn't have enough faith in divine providence. The principal of Villa Notre-Dame had often advised her, "Count your blessings!"

"I've got nothing to complain about, really," she said to Annette. "It's heaven here."

"Well, it seems like it."

They weren't used to the feeling of exultation that arose in them every morning when they left the yard and walked down to the cathedral to attend mass. They didn't go in a group, but in twos or threes, with companions of their own choice. They could talk and laugh as much as they wanted, like normal girls. And if they sometimes perceived in the looks of the nuns the message *Don't expect special treatment because you're the Dionne quintuplets,* it only made them happier. Being treated like all the others was exactly what they wanted!

Little by little, each quint learned to separate herself from the others, to lead a life that was a bit different from her sisters' — especially Marie, whose spirit of independence was blossoming and who showed no more interest in religious life. This process was made easier by the fact that they slept in one big dormitory and could be together as often as they wanted. Here, no one scolded them when they formed a group apart; no one was worried that they were telling secrets. Because they were free to establish the intimacy that had been denied them in the past, each discovered the further pleasure of flying with her own wings and developing her own personality. Émilie was often sick, and her bed became the place where the quints gathered; she welcomed them back to the nest after their adventures in the new world around them.

The quints thought that the nuns were a little strict with them sometimes, and they worried that the slightest deviation from the rules on their part would be reported to their father. It was as if, at any moment, their mother might poke her finger between their shoulder blades and prod, "Sit up straight. Don't do this! Don't do that!"

They felt their father's hold over them every Sunday afternoon, when they were locked into an empty classroom while their classmates received visitors. This order could only have come from him, and it took them back to the days of being closed in behind fences.

They took advantage of this forced isolation to get through a weekly chore: writing the obligatory letters to their parents. This was no simple task, however. Each word had to be weighed, each sentence analyzed, because their father was very good at reading between the lines. Too short a letter would make him angry; too happy a letter would unsettle him. If they were too vague, he would be sure they were hiding something. Their letters had to express how much they missed home and their warm feelings for the family — but they mustn't overdo it, or their father would doubt their sincerity.

Marie and Yvonne compared the letters that they had just finished.

"You forgot to ask about Lucie," Yvonne noted, handing the letter back to her sister.

"Would a P.S. be enough?"

"Oh, yes. I ask at the beginning. He'll average things out."

All five laughed uneasily.

"I feel like a hypocrite," Annette admitted.

"They're forcing us to do it," Marie replied sharply.

Émilie grunted in agreement.

"It's not hypocrisy," Cécile said, "it's simple courtesy. We don't offend them. They're happy. It's diplomatic and it avoids complications for us."

Although she knew she was right, the letters that Cécile wrote every week weighed heavily on her conscience, not because she was lying — she knew she had to protect herself — but because it reminded her of her inability to love her family as she should. She attributed this shortcoming to a detestable egoism, which she frequently admitted at confession and tried to correct in herself.

While the others read to kill time until supper, Marie looked out the window at visitors coming and going, at groups of students and parents strolling down the paths, and she imagined the bursts of laughter that the window panes kept her from hearing. *It must be nice to want to see your family*, she thought. In the adjacent park, the maples had lost their fiery colors, and the few leaves that were still clinging to branches were a dull brown. It reminded her of Corbeil, where autumn was the color of rust.

"Do you remember the 'little room' in the nursery?" she asked.

"Vaguely," Annette said.

At The Dafoe Hospital and Nursery, corporal punishment had been forbidden. When one of them had done something wrong, the nurses put the guilty party in a tiny room, no bigger than a cupboard, containing just a chair, a table, and a window.

"The worst part of it," Yvonne said, "was being separated. The others suffered as much as the one who was in the little room."

"It's so long ago," Émilie sighed. "Sometimes, I feel like it was another life, and someone else who lived through it."

"We were happy," Marie said. "I remember that! They should have left us in the hospital, with the nurses. The reunion wasn't good for anyone, not the family and not us."

Émilie put down her book. "I want to turn over a new leaf," she said.

"How do we do that?" Yvonne asked skeptically.

"Maybe the first step is to forgive them."

"And how do we do that, Em?"

Émilie didn't know what to say. She picked up her book and pretended to read, but the question continued to turn around in her head.

"Prayer," Marie suggested. "I think that's the only way."

"Lots of prayers!" said Annette sardonically.

• • •

A visit by their father and mother in mid October caught the quintuplets by surprise. Their alarm was unfounded, however, for their parents hadn't come to take them home. Elzire simply wanted to see how the girls were doing. Their time together was strained. They had little to tell each other; most of the news about family and school had already been exchanged in letters. As they spoke, the girls weighed their words as carefully as they did in their letters, for they never knew what would make their

155

parents angry. They told Elzire and Oliva about Monseigneur Tessier's visit, three days earlier, at which they had sung, and about the banquet for the Virgin that was coming up in November.

Elzire and Oliva's visit reminded the quints that they weren't all that far away from Corbeil, after all, and that their independence was still an aspiration, not a reality. Christmas vacation wasn't far off, and they would be returning home for the holidays. They had to make the most of their time in Nicolet, since their mother might get a strange idea into her head, or their father might change his mind all of a sudden, and their still-fragile liberty would vanish in an instant.

Two weeks later, Cécile and Yvonne decided that it would be nice to go to town on Saturday afternoon, as most of the girls did. They asked for permission, as they had been taught to do — and, to their great astonishment, they received it. Their father must have forgotten to forbid these outings, or else the nun wasn't aware of his instructions, or perhaps she had forgotten them. They wouldn't bother to mention it in their next letter . . .

For this first foray into the outside world, Yvonne and Cécile didn't stray far from the school — there were so many new things to see and do! Once they got over their nervousness, they enjoyed their anonymity: there were no photographers dogging their every step, no one telling them where to go.

"This is just the beginning!" Cécile said. "Someday . . ."

Eventually, they went into a music store to check out the latest recordings. When they heard the first measures of "Cinq Jumelles," a song about them, they realized that the saleslady knew who they were, and they quickly left. But in spite of this, the adventure went well, and they

156

told their sisters all about it. Yvonne and Cécile had established a precedent; now they could all feel free to go to town whenever they felt brave enough.

One thing these outings made them realize was that they had no money. Their father paid them an allowance of two dollars per month, which was just enough to pay for the pencils and notebooks they needed. Compared to the other girls, they were poor!

Not having the courage to ask their father to increase their allowance, they mentioned their problem instead to the principal, who was surprised.

"Just two dollars? But you're rich enough to buy the whole school if you wanted!"

She promised to intervene. The following month each girl's allowance was raised to five dollars. But they pondered for a long time what the principal had said. What exactly had she meant? Was their father a wealthy man? How did this stranger know what his own daughters didn't?

"There's nothing surprising about it," Annette concluded after they had mulled it over for the twentieth time. "They never tell us anything."

"I'd say they're keeping something from us," Marie added.

They thought about Émilie's epilepsy, which the family kept hidden as if it were a shameful defect, and about the affection and happiness that they simulated in front of strangers. What else was being concealed? Although they had no doubt that it concerned them, they decided it was better not to dig too deep.

"Lucie and the others know what's going on, but they don't tell us anything," Annette said.

"Especially when it has to do with money," Émilie added, with a mocking look.

"I'm not surprised. I still have trouble telling a nickel from a quarter!"

• • •

When the holidays finally came, the quintuplets took the train home for Christmas. They all felt a creeping anxiety — not because they were traveling alone for the first time, but because they were thinking about their destination. They wanted to believe that their absence had solved the family's problems, that their reunion would be joyful, that their stay in the big house would be peaceful and pleasant. They wanted to believe it, but couldn't. And their worry grew as the journey came to an end.

Cécile glanced apprehensively at Émilie, who was sleeping with her head on her shoulder. She had prayed so many times that everything would go well in Corbeil, she had tried so hard to convince herself, that from time to time she managed to feel sincere pleasure at the idea of seeing some members of her family. But the certainty that she would be the target of cutting remarks, that she would be witness to, if not the object of, the usual arguments, ruined what happiness she felt. "They" would not have changed; she herself had not changed as much as she would have liked. It was impossible to forget nine years of bullying and constant anxiety. Even at Nicolet, a vague threat hung over Cécile; she was plagued with a feeling of impending doom.

She glanced over at her other sisters: Annette was sleeping, Marie was reading a magazine. Sensing Cécile's eyes upon her, Yvonne turned away from the window, and Cécile could see the stress on her face. She opened her mouth to say something, but just at that moment a group of revelers wandering from car to car recognized

158

the famous quintuplets. They stopped and stared at them unabashedly. Like most travelers, they were no doubt on their way to see family and friends. The train had a festive ambiance from which the quints felt totally excluded.

Once the curious crowd had gone, Marie sighed. "I wish the holiday were over!" she said to Cécile.

When they finally arrived at the "big house," sitting in a thick carpet of snow, it seemed even more austere than they remembered it.

"They look like pairs of empty eyes," Émilie said, pointing to the windows.

They went in by the side door. The moment they were inside the kitchen, they put on all their old habits, the same way their mother put on her apron. The visit would be exactly as they had imagined.

• • •

Five months later, Elzire and Oliva Dionne went to Nicolet for the quintuplets' nineteenth birthday. The nuns provided them with a cottage beside the Institute. After the usual photo session for the press, the quints and their parents found themselves alone in a pretty but impersonal living room.

"It smells clean," Elzire noted with satisfaction.

"It smells like the convent," Oliva said flatly. The big smile that he had worn for the photographers was gone. In the same neutral, implacable voice, he asked his daughters, "Are you happy here?"

"Oh, yes," Annette hurriedly replied. "Thank you for sending us here. We know it must be very expensive."

Fearing that her sister's words might be misinterpreted, Cécile added, "But we miss you and Mom, and the house."

Elzire smiled happily. "In less than a month you'll be home for the summer. I can't wait."

As she spoke, she looked at each of her daughters in turn. Her smile vanished when her eyes fell on Émilie. Nobody missed this, least of all Émilie. Silence fell, and it seemed to last an eternity. In less than a month . . . The quints were only too well aware of it!

To dissipate the strained atmosphere, Yvonne told her parents about her progress in cooking — she who so detested home economics. Her sisters made similar speeches, and then they asked about the other members of the family. Neither mother nor daughters were fooled by this bit of play-acting. Annette told herself that their parents weren't looking forward to their homecoming any more than they were. So why were they carrying on this charade? Who were they trying to fool?

His face impassive, Oliva did not join in the conversation. *Two years from now*, he was thinking, *my little girls will be adults, and their money will be theirs by right. There are complications on the horizon . . .*

Once all the news of family and acquaintances had been exchanged, silence fell once again. But before it became oppressive, Marie stood up.

"I have an announcement to make."

Her parents gave her an uneasy look, and her sisters wondered what it could be, since she hadn't mentioned anything to them. Fragile and usually shy, Marie bore the others' looks without flinching, as if an inner strength were lending her courage.

"I am going to enter a convent and devote myself to the service of God. I've thought about this for a long time, I've prayed, and I've made my decision."

Émilie, Annette, Yvonne, and Cécile were dumfounded,

but Elzire beamed with joy, clasping her hands together.

"Oh, you've made me so happy! Every family should have at least one vocation. The Sisters of the Assumption?"

"No. The Servants of the Very Holy Sacrament in Quebec City."

"Cloistered?" Émilie cried, dreading the prospect of never seeing her beloved sister again except through a grille.

"Yes. I will pray for the salvation of the world."

"That's good," Elzire said. "There are so many people, starting with your own family, who prayed for a miracle to keep you alive! You will return their prayers. That's perfect."

Marie glanced anxiously at her sisters, who had not yet reacted. She quickly realized that as their shock wore off, it was their disapproval that kept them from speaking. A shadow fell over her face, and the other four immediately went to kiss her and offer their congratulations.

"We'll celebrate this at the same time as your birthday!" Elzire said merrily. "When are you entering the convent?"

"In September!" decreed Oliva, unclenching his teeth for the first time since Marie had announced her decision. Even more than his stony face, his cold, expressionless voice cloaked his feelings on the subject.

"Oh, Dad, you know I won't change my mind."

"Not before September! Until then, not a word about this to anyone. We'll all keep it a secret."

Uncomprehendingly, his wife and daughters agreed. This wasn't like him — it would make such good fodder for the press!

In fact, he didn't really know how to react under the circumstances. It was so sudden, so unforeseen. And such news had be exploited judiciously for publicity purposes.

161

Émilie was happy that her father had put off the date to the fall. This would give her two more months of Marie's presence. Perhaps she could change her mind.

Because the kitchen in the cottage was small, Elzire kept only Marie to help her make dinner. Once they had set the table, the other four went outside to take a short walk. Without saying a word, they made their way down the dirt road that snaked through the fields behind the Institute. Baptized "Pouletteville" by the students — no one knew why — it was their favorite place to take a stroll. It was here that Cécile had dared to ask a nun whom she trusted two questions that had haunted her for a long time. Had the fact that they had been fed milk from black women soon after their birth marked their bodies? And was it a sin to love one's parents only to obey God's commandment that ordered them to do it, without it coming naturally from the heart? To both questions, Sister Léon had answered, with her usual gentleness and comprehension, "No."

When she found the forget-me-nots that she'd been looking for, Cécile no longer felt like picking them for a bouquet, as she had intended to. Suddenly, they seemed too fragile and delicate to be appreciated by her mother.

Yvonne walked with her head down, unaware of her surroundings. She envied Marie's courage. Marie hadn't said "I want to" or "I'd like to." She'd said "I am entering the convent." She had said "I've made my decision," and the roof hadn't fallen in. *Does that mean I might be able to do what I want the most?* Yvonne wondered. In any case, she wouldn't bring it up today; it wasn't the time. She might spoil Marie's plans. There would be another opportunity.

"It doesn't make sense!" Émilie exclaimed as soon as

she was out of earshot of the cottage. "I can't see her in a cloister."

"Me neither," Annette said. "She's going to turn her back on the world before she even knows what it is."

Cécile sighed deeply and said, defeated, "It's easy to let go of what you don't have."

"But she's letting go of us!" Émilie wailed. "What will I do? I thought we were never going to leave each other."

Yvonne turned her head with a twinge of guilt. Since she was thinking of going off on her own, she felt bound to defend Marie's decision. "It's not a question of abandoning anyone. Peewee is answering a call. It's not just her right to do it, it's her duty."

"But she never discussed it with us!" Annette said sadly. "I would have told her to think long and hard about it."

"No doubt that's what she wanted to avoid. We might have tried to make her change her mind. We have to respect her decision."

In spite of Yvonne's firm tone, Émilie wasn't convinced. "Her decision? It's not as final as that! And she just happened to choose the cloister where she went on closed retreat with Lucie a few weeks ago. Lucie influenced her, I'm sure of it. She told her to go into the cloister and leave everybody else in peace!"

Émilie was trembling with an unaccustomed rage. Worried that it would provoke an epileptic seizure, Cécile put her arm around her and pulled her close, trying to calm her down.

"Why would Lucie want to do that?"

"Just for the satisfaction of separating us, dividing us up!"

"Come on, Em, you know Marie better than that. She wouldn't let herself be swayed like that. Remember, we've all thought of entering a convent."

"Peewee isn't the type to be a nun," Émilie pleaded. "And cloistered on top of it all! She's not healthy enough for that life."

"That's true," Cécile admitted. Getting hold of herself, she added, "We have to let her try things on her own. *They've* always told us what to do. *They've* always made our decisions. We shouldn't do that to each other."

Yvonne went over to Émilie and gently stroked the nape of her neck. "Cis is right, Em. We have to respect Peewee's wish, and even find a way to support her."

"Respect it, yes, but encourage it? That's too much to ask of me."

"You won't be alone. You'll have us, Annette, Cécile, and me."

"I have a feeling you're all going to go off on your own," Émilie said sadly. "First, Peewee. Who's next?"

She examined her sisters' faces, stopping longest at Yvonne, who had trouble meeting her gaze. Émilie began to say something, but at that very moment Marie called them in for dinner.

"Let's not spoil Peewee's joy," Cécile recommended. "Let's all smile."

Émilie lagged behind the others, trying to compose a calm face. When she realized this, Annette slowed down to wait for her. When Émilie caught up, Annette gave her a pat on the shoulder.

"We'll stay with you, Em. Anyway, Quebec City isn't the end of the world. We'll go visit Marie often."

"We'll see her through a grille," Émilie muttered bitterly. "Yvonne is planning something, too. Has she said anything to you, Netta?"

"No."

7

Oliva Dionne was pleased. All the reporters he'd expected were gathered in the big living room of his house in Corbeil. They had come from as far away as Toronto, Montreal, and Quebec City. He cleared his throat to silence the last whispers.

"For a number of years now, an idea has been growing in little Marie's head and heart. It was something she did not dare share with her mother and father, fearing that we would oppose her. All my decisions have always been made in the best interests of the quintuplets. That is still true today. So, I feel I should not thwart Marie's most cherished wish. Any questions?"

Like his statement, all of Oliva's responses had been prepared in advance, since he knew what the reporters would ask. It was habit. Even when a reporter asked if he could hear Marie's version of the story, Oliva was not taken by surprise.

Marie knew what she had to say. She stood up from the chair where she had been sitting beside her mother.

Her hands clasped so that no one would see that they were trembling, she said, with a conviction that masked her shyness, "I am very grateful to all the people all over the world who prayed for my sisters and me when we were babies. I want to return this faith from which we benefited. From now on, all my prayers will be for them."

When she'd finished, a reporter asked, "How do you feel about being separated from your sisters?"

"I will suffer greatly, but I will offer this sacrifice to God. It will be another way of praying for the world."

Marie's words rang with such conviction that any further questions seemed inappropriate. In any case, her father had already supplied all the useful information and necessary explanations. They had already taken the photographs that would accompany their articles, all carefully posed, of Elzire Dionne helping her daughter pack her bags, Marie kneeling before her father as he gave her his blessing, and Oliva and Elzire bidding farewell to their daughter on the front steps of the big house.

One week before Marie left for the convent in Quebec City, there was a big party at the Dionne home for family and friends. The only people missing were Émilie, Annette, Yvonne, and Cécile, since it was mid September and they had already returned to boarding school. In any case, they hadn't been told about it.

Her sisters' absence suited Marie; it would have been hard for her to bear the sadness that they would have not been able to hide from her. Above all, there would have been Émilie's reproachful eyes. Her favorite sister had been making her silent plea all summer, a plea that had grown insistent as their separation drew nearer. Marie was joyful to be giving herself to God, and she bitterly regretted that her vocation was causing Émilie so much pain. It would have been so good to take this step with more serenity. Marie had stretched the truth for the reporters: it was her sisters, especially Émilie, for whom she would pray the most.

● ● ●

While Elzire and Marie went inside the convent of the Servants of the Very Holy Sacrament to take care of the final formalities, Yvonne, Cécile, and Annette walked along the neighboring streets. They thought that they would have a lot to say to each other, since they hadn't been all together for several weeks.

In fact, Yvonne was keeping to herself. Thanks to Lucie's intervention, she had won her father's permission to attend Marguerite-Bourgeoys College in Montreal. To explain her desire for an education that would lead to art school, Yvonne had spoken of her passion for painting and her total lack of interest in cooking and home economics. She had been careful not to mention to Oliva that she would also be taking the chemistry course she would need for admission to nursing school later on.

In the end, the three sisters walked in silence, for the move that Marie was making today seemed to make any other topic of conversation irrelevant. When they returned to the cloister, they saw dozens of reporters and photographers standing guard in front of the austere yellow-brick building.

"Them again!" Yvonne muttered.

Annette simply nodded her head. These last few weeks, intrigued by the news of Marie entering the convent, the newspapers were hungry for more stories on the Dionne quintuplets.

"I wish they would forget about us a little bit," Yvonne said, slowing down.

"*Someone* is making sure that doesn't happen." Cécile's caustic tone betrayed the tension she was feeling. That someone, of course, was their father.

Annette squeezed Cécile's arm reassuringly. Over the last few days, they had discussed Marie's decision at length. Although they did not believe it was for the best, they had prayed for God to light her way. Annette glanced quickly at Cécile; her withdrawn expression, which others might attribute to the solemnity of the event, was actually a look of worry.

"Stop torturing yourself, Cis. You've said it often enough: Marie has to do what she thinks is best."

"It's not that, Netta. I'm worried about Émilie, all alone in Nicolet."

"The nuns will take good care of her."

Annette said this as much to convince herself as to calm Cécile. She could not forget Émilie's tears when they had said goodbye, but she would have cried just as much watching Marie take the veil.

"She was already taking Marie's leaving badly," Cécile said. "Not letting her come to Quebec City today was inhuman!"

Their mother had come to get them at Nicolet after picking up Yvonne in Montreal, and she had refused to let Émilie make the trip. Deaf to her daughters' pleas, Elzire had decreed, "It will be too emotional for you. You'll get sick. I don't want you to make me ashamed in front of the reporters in Quebec City."

Although Yvonne didn't join in her sisters' conversation, she was following it with interest. She, too, wondered whether Marie was doing the right thing, but

168

still, it made her feel a bit better. She could always tell herself that she had not been the one to break up their "family"; Marie had gone first.

Alone in a strange city, Yvonne missed her sisters terribly and wrote to them every week. But at least this separation had a goal that gave her pain a purpose. It was different for Émilie. She was suffering through the successive departures of Marie and Yvonne; of course she felt abandoned.

"Are you taking good care of her?" she asked them.

"It's all right, Ivy," Annette said reassuringly. "We're looking out for her. They've given her a room in the nuns' wing, and Cis stays with her."

Annette's affectionate look when she said these words was a true balm for Yvonne's troubled soul. She had understood what Annette was really saying: *Do what you must, and we'll take care of Émilie. Later, when you can, it will be your turn.* All three were certain that their sister, with her fragile health, was not yet able to face life alone. One or the other would keep her under their wing, as long as she needed it.

As they made their way through the crowd of reporters in front of the gate, they ran a gauntlet of questions and flashbulbs. They lowered their eyes and walked more quickly, but the reporters persisted.

Tired of fighting, Cécile turned to face them. "We are all very happy that Marie has found her way," she stated, giving the other two time to slip inside.

In the entrance hall, Yvonne, Annette, and Cécile joined their mother. For some reason, their father had not made the trip, leaving it to one of his sons-in-law to drive Elzire and Marie. Also present was a reporter from the newspaper *La Patrie*, who was enjoying this special favor because he had once provided Oliva with valuable assistance in his battle against Dr. Dafoe and the Ontario government. The embraces were brief, for the nuns had gathered and lined up in a double row.

"Miss Marie, a last statement for our readers before you retreat into silence?" the reporter asked.

Elzire gave her permission with a nod of her head. Marie turned to the reporter. Her expression was serious and her voice was composed and sure: "Worldly affairs don't interest me. I feel that my place is in this convent. It's the only place where I can be happy."

As she talked, she looked not at the reporter but at her three sisters, to make them understand that her decision was irrevocable and fulfilled an intense desire. Above all, she wanted them not to be angry with her. A shiver ran down Annette's spine; she envied Marie her determination. In the end, Marie was lucky: she had found her path in life. It didn't matter that the existence she had chosen was harsh and reclusive. The certainty itself must have been a source of inner peace. Not knowing was really the hard part.

Moving awkwardly, her face beaming with pride, Elzire led her daughter over to the nuns. Without a gesture or look of farewell, Marie stepped between the nuns and walked down the corridor made of human walls. With every step, she was separating herself from the world, distancing herself from her past, giving it up forever. Like the wings of a gate, the two lines of veiled women closed behind her frail silhouette.

Her heart tight with loss, Cécile could not keep back her tears. She told herself that Émilie could not have borne this scene without collapsing. Yvonne and Annette were crying, too; even Elzire's eyes were wet. In the depths of the cloister, novices helped Marie to shed her city clothes and don a black habit, while Elzire and her daughters waited in a tiny parlor. The three quints stared at each other, overwhelmed.

"How does it feel to lose a daughter like this, Mrs. Dionne?" the reporter asked.

"I'm not losing her, since she is giving herself to God. On the contrary, our family is gaining a nun."

"Émilie isn't here. Is she sick?"

They heard suspicion in the reporter's voice. Elzire jerked her chin toward Annette. Taken by surprise, Annette searched for words that would not betray their secret.

Cécile came to her rescue, lying with aplomb. "She's not sick, Mr. Legris. She's injured."

"It must be serious for her not to be able to come and say goodbye to Marie."

"She hurt her ankle running, and she can't walk at the moment."

"A fracture?" he said, scribbling in his notebook.

"No, just a sprain."

Confronted with Cécile's firm voice and curt answers, he realized that his questions would not garner much information, unless he found a way to throw her off balance. But he wouldn't do that to the Dionne family, who had often opened their door to him, especially when it concerned one of the quintuplets. In any case, it was not the right time for such a gambit.

After a wait that seemed interminable, the heavy black wooden grille opened to reveal Marie, almost unrecognizable in the white veil of a postulant. Annette realized that the habit had not changed her sister; it was a new serenity that had transfigured her face. She knew that she couldn't stay angry at Marie.

The goodbyes took just a few minutes, and the words exchanged were ordinary. What started with smiles ended with hugs and silent tears. Just before she disappeared, Marie kissed each of her sisters in turn.

"Until you take your vows, nothing is final," Yvonne whispered. "If you're not happy here . . ."

"I already am, Ivy, and I hope you'll find total happiness too."

Cécile heard what Yvonne had said; it was what she herself would have told her sister. So she just murmured, "Good luck, my beautiful Marie."

"You will keep an eye on my dear Émilie, won't you?" Marie's tone betrayed her anxiety, a crack in the mask of tranquil confidence that she had worn up to now.

"You can count on us. We won't leave her."

"Of course. Pardon me. I don't even know why I asked."

"Because you love her as much as we do."

They squeezed each other's hands and then separated. Annette was so moved that she joked as she kissed Marie, "The habit makes you look different. With your thick soles, you're taller than me! Will you keep a little place for me in your prayers?"

"Do you want me to pray for you to get taller?"

This repartee reassured Annette: although Marie had heard God's call, she had not lost her sense of humor. The veil and habit would not be able to extinguish her love of life.

"Pray that I find my path, too."

Then the wooden grille opened once more, and Marie joined her new family, walking away without the strength to cast a last glance at what she was leaving behind.

Cécile, Yvonne, and Annette huddled together, needing

172

human warmth. Frozen to the spot, they listened to the echo of their sister's footsteps fade away. Cécile and Yvonne found it inconceivable that Marie was to be enclosed forever behind this grille, walled up in this cold stone convent, when outside there was a world that they had yet to discover. Having lived so long behind fences, how could she choose deliberately to shut herself in a prison?

Annette knew that she had lost Marie once and for all. Gone forever were the friendship, secrets, laughs, and games that they had shared. Their life as quintuplets would have to be carried on by the remaining four. They would have to continue dealing with it and trying to understand it without Marie's help. Whenever she saw her sister from now on, it would no longer be Marie before her, but a nun, whose concerns had nothing in common with her own. Annette guessed that Émilie, who had been the closest to Marie, was thinking the same thing.

Elzire's voice made them jump: "All right, let's go!"

● ● ●

A cotton curtain served as the door to the tiny cell where Marie slept on a straw pallet on the floor. The rough sheets, a nun explained, were a silent reminder of the vows she would one day take. And so that the postulants would not develop a sentimental attachment to these walls, as impersonal as they were, they regularly changed cells. Marie was allowed to keep one souvenir of her old life: a photograph of her family. She avoided looking at it; the smiles of her sisters seemed forced, and the photograph made her remember how hard they'd tried to hide their sadness over her decision to enter the convent.

In any case, she didn't need to look at it: her sisters were always in her thoughts, even when she tried to lose herself in prayer.

The days flowed by, in a rhythm dictated by the bells summoning her to prayer or to work. The community's rules determined the conduct of the nuns down to the smallest detail, ordered how they spent their hours, and excluded any frivolous occupations. The slightest hesitation in obeying the call of the bells, the smallest deviation from the rules, and the most involuntary distractions were noted by Marie in the notebook in which she listed her weaknesses. All the postulants kept such a list; it was one more way of learning to abandon themselves totally to the will of God.

With the exception of half-hour recreation periods after lunch and supper, absolute silence reigned in the cloister. When communication was absolutely necessary, the nuns used hand signals; otherwise, they kept their eyes down and their hands hidden in the sleeves of their habit.

It was quite easy for Marie to get used to living without talking, but there was no silence within her. After months of an existence dedicated entirely to adoration of the holy sacrament and prayer, she still heard voices. Detachment from the world and from loved ones, she realized, was something she had yet to achieve, although she thought she had done so when she took the veil; it hurt her as if she were cutting into her own flesh. Although she could write only two letters a month, she could receive an unlimited number, and every one of her sisters' letters revived a pain that she thought she had driven away through superhuman effort. She offered this test of separation to God, asking Him to deliver her from it as soon as possible.

174

Forgetting the world of nature was not easy, either. Every time she passed a window, she was sorely tempted to lift her eyes to see the blue sky and the clouds floating by. Running through the trees, lying in the grass, listening to the birds singing, plunging her nose into a flower: these were the guilty fantasies that disturbed her sometimes during her devotions, and they were duly noted in the notebook.

In spite of these difficulties, Marie did not for an instant doubt the authenticity of her vocation. Practicing poverty, chastity, and obedience was easy for her, confirming that she was committed to the path that God had chosen for her.

● ● ●

The months passed, but the quintuplets could not get used to living apart from one another, one in Montreal, three in Nicolet, and one in Quebec City. Letters flew back and forth, often crossing in transit, and they visited each other as often as possible.

In May 1954, a few days before their twentieth birthday, Émilie, Annette, Yvonne, and Cécile were together in the chapel of the cloistered convent of the Servants of the Very Holy Sacrament to watch their sister take her first vows. Accepted by the congregation after a trial period as a postulant, Marie was becoming a novice and taking the name Sister Marie-Rachel; in two years, she would take her perpetual vows.

At the end of the school year, Annette, Cécile, and Émilie returned home to Corbeil. Yvonne would join them as soon as her exams were over. The atmosphere was not as tense in the house, since many of their brothers and sisters had left home. Their mother scolded them

175

less harshly than before and no longer hit them, and their father was less strict. Nevertheless, the climate of mistrust had become even more oppressive. Elzire and Oliva seemed to be feeling a profound disappointment and rancor toward the quints that could not be explained.

A few days after they arrived in the big house, Émilie asked Cécile and Annette to go out and pick strawberries with her. It was more a demand than a request, and her unusually firm tone surprised her sisters.

"Was this Mom's idea?" Annette asked. "Is she coming, too?"

"No, just the three of us. I have something to tell you."

Another surprise? Émilie, who was not very open by nature, had withdrawn even more since Marie had entered the convent.

"Let's go right now, before the sun is too strong," Cécile suggested, realizing that this was important to Émilie. Because they shared a room at Nicolet, she had learned to interpret her sister's hesitations, silences, and tone of voice. This time, however, she had no idea what Émilie was feeling or thinking.

"It was in the month of May . . ." Annette began to sing as they passed the barn and went out into the field, where a dozen sheep were grazing.

Émilie joined in the song. Cécile, uneasy, did not have the heart to sing; as she walked, she glanced distractedly at the white tufts of daisies among the orange hawkweed. Had Émilie been molested by their father again? Each trip to the house in Corbeil was more difficult than the last, for the very walls of the big house reminded Cécile of a horrible part of her life. The summer holidays weighed heavily upon her. She couldn't wait for September!

176

"It seems strange — just the three of us," Annette said after a few minutes.

"The five of us will never be together again." Émilie said these words flatly — she who had once so dreaded the idea that they might one day be separated. Her depression over Marie's departure had hung on for several weeks. Cécile was more and more intrigued by her sister's attitude.

"It's true that Marie won't ever leave the cloister again," Annette answered, "but we can all go and see her, like we did in May."

She thought about the ceremony they had attended in Quebec City. All five of them had been in the chapel, but a world had separated Marie from her sisters.

"You're right, Em," Annette added. "Things will never be the same again."

Instead of stopping in the meadow, where strawberries were growing in profusion, Émilie led the others to the edge of the woods.

"This is good," she said, sitting down in the sparse shade of an aspen. Then she looked around at the tender green of the woods around them. "In the middle of the good Lord's great nature," she added, "this is the right place."

Suddenly, Cécile knew what Émilie was going to tell them. And she didn't know if she could be happy for her.

"A bobolink!" Annette cried, pointing to a bird with a black chest and a creamy neck perched on a fencepost.

"I could never live without nature's beauty," Émilie responded. "In Nicolet, I missed it terribly . . ." The sentence left unfinished and the way her voice trailed off told Cécile that Émilie was about to get to the point. With a wave of her hand, she gestured for Annette to be quiet.

"We're listening, Em."

Émilie gave her sisters a long look and smiled broadly. "I'm entering a convent."

Annette kept herself from exclaiming, "You too!" and asked instead, "Which convent?"

"The Warm Welcome Hospice, in Sainte-Agathe."

Like her sisters, Cécile had heard about this institution, founded by Father Parent, an oblate who had often visited them at Villa Notre-Dame. It was a retirement home for aged priests, run by nuns.

"Do you know what you're doing, Em?" Cécile asked gently.

"I thought about it all winter," Émilie said happily, "and I've made my decision."

"I don't know what Mom and Dad will say," Annette murmured, taken aback by her sister's decision.

"Oh!" Émilie had thought that it would please them. They must have been scared that one day she would come home to stay, along with her illness, which they found so horrifying. She added, simply, "No one can make me change my mind."

Annette realized that she had not yet congratulated Émilie. She kissed her on both cheeks. Cécile followed suit, but with an awkwardness that did not escape Émilie's notice. She asked, a little anxiously, "Do you think I'm making a mistake?"

"No," Annette said. "I'm surprised, that's all. You have to admit, Em, it's sudden. You never talked about it."

"I didn't want to say anything until I was sure. I discussed it a lot with my guardian of conscience."

As Émilie described the large white house in the heart of the Laurentians, with many windows looking out on a peaceful, natural setting, Cécile was surprised that she hadn't suspected anything before now. Lately, Émilie always had her nose in a book about the history of the Church or the lives of the saints, but she had been reading these types of books since she turned thirteen. She prayed a lot, but then, she had always been very religious. And she had never shown any interest in nice clothes or boys, nor had she ever worn make-up.

"I would like to live without attachments, be a child in the woods. Nature means so much to me. Do you remember, I wrote that in a composition a long time ago. They weren't empty words. I've never stopped thinking about it."

"All that counts," Cécile told her, "is for you to be happy."

"And I am, Cis, I always will be. 'The Lord is my shepherd . . .'"

"I remember back when you were just fifteen, you were already dreaming of being a nun," Annette said.

"Maybe I was already hearing the call from afar. You know I have great hearing!" she teased. Then she said, seriously, "Deep within me, I always knew I would devote my life to God."

Cécile reflected on what this would mean in practical terms. Would their parents accept it? If they refused, the quints would have to stick together and stand up to them, convince them to give in. Yvonne would have to come quickly from Montreal. She would be thunderstruck, too.

"It would be better if you didn't approach it that way with Mom and Dad," she advised Émilie. "Don't say it's for life. Say that you want to try, that you want to be a postulant like Marie, to see if it's the right life for you."

"All right."

"Are you sure they'll take you?" Annette asked.

"I write to Father Parent regularly," Émilie replied, smiling confidently.

"In that case," Cécile concluded with a little laugh, "all we have to do is take you to Sainte-Agathe."

"With two nuns praying for me now, I'm sure I'll figure out what to do with my life!" Annette exclaimed. When she was thirteen, Annette had dreamed of escaping, but now that freedom was within her grasp, she didn't know what to do. She was the only one of the quints who still didn't have a clear idea about her future.

Émilie squeezed her hand. "Patience, Annette. God will tell you." She looked at Cécile and said, "If you want to make me happy, let's kneel under this tree, in the great church of the world, and pray together for Marie to get strong and Yvonne to pass her exams."

"And for Netta to find her way," Cécile joked as she knelt on the grass that was so well trimmed by sheep.

• • •

Serving God by taking care of his aged and ill priests filled Émilie with joy and peace. And in this house, nestled in steep hills among twisted spruce trees, she felt as though she had arrived at her destination at last. Here, she could forget about the outside world and be reborn with another name. To cut herself off from the past and feel free, all she needed to do was forgive the evil that had been done to her.

Thinking of her sisters did not bother Émilie. She missed them, of course, but, paradoxically, it was a serene feeling. She had no anxiety for Marie, whose too-rare letters testified that she had found happiness in the cloister. As for Yvonne, Annette, and Cécile, they were strong and would figure out how to get along by themselves.

"It's nice to hear you sing, Émilie. You fill the house with joy."

180

Public opinion was of primary importance to Oliva Dionne.
He took advantage of the smallest event to keep the Dionne name in the media.
Émilie, Yvonne, Annette, Marie, and Cécile (l. to r.) learned how to
behave in front of the camera when they were very young.

*Cécile, Émilie, Yvonne, Annette, Marie, and their father
read Cardinal Spellman's invitation.*

*In the living room of the family home, Émilie, Cécile,
and Yvonne (sitting), and Marie and Annette (standing with
their mother between them), at sixteen years old.*

During a visit to Canada, Princess Elizabeth and the Duke of Edinburgh
stopped over in North Bay, where they were introduced to
Yvonne, Annette, Émilie, Marie, and Cécile (l. to r.).

At Oliva Dionne's request, nuns from Sturgeon Falls organized an official graduation ceremony at the end of high school. Decorators from Bannon Bros. built a stage in the basement playroom of the Dionne house. The event took place on the eighteenth birthday of Cécile, Yvonne, Marie, Annette, and Émilie (l. to r.), photographed with their mother.

Émilie, Yvonne, Cécile, Annette, and Marie (l. to r.) rarely went unnoticed when they ventured out. Their new photographer came from New York at regular intervals to take press photographs.

*In October 1950, a large crowd gathered on the platform at Grand Central
Station in New York to see Cécile, Annette, Yvonne, Marie, and Émilie (l. to r.)
off. During this trip, the quints attended, among other events,
the annual $100-a-plate banquet for the Alfred E. Smith Foundation.*

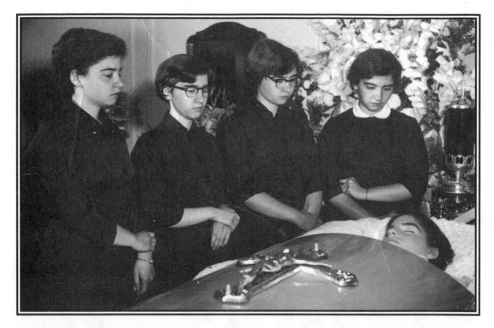

Cécile, Marie, Yvonne, and Annette (l. to r.) with the remains of Émilie, deceased at the age of twenty years, two months, and twelve days.

On May 28, 1955, Marie places a bouquet on Émilie's grave in the Corbeil cemetery, as Yvonne, Cécile, and Annette (l. to r.) look on.

Marie's flower shop, which opened in May 1956,
quickly became her sisters' project too.

None of their classmates were the least bit envious of the celebrity
of Yvonne, Annette, Marie, Cécile, and Émilie (l. to r.)
when they went to New York in October 1950.

She jumped, not having heard anyone come, and turned away from the bed she was making. One of the nuns was standing in the doorway, smiling.

"There's a telephone call for you, Émilie. It's about your sister."

Which one? Émilie wondered as she ran for the telephone on the ground floor. Something serious must be happening in Corbeil for them to call her in the middle of the afternoon, when the long-distance rates were higher than in the evening.

"Hello?" she said anxiously.

"Hello, Émilie. It's Father Parent."

"Oh, hello, Father."

Émilie's relief was short-lived. The priest told her that, at Marie's request, he had gone to get her in Quebec City and had taken her to the convent of the oblates, in Richelieu.

"What's wrong, Father? Is she sick?"

"It's exhaustion, mostly. Nothing that should worry you, my daughter. I believe that the cloistered life is too hard on Marie. It's ruining her health. Here, she will rest and regain her strength. She would like to see you."

"Yes, I must go to her. Is it possible, Father?"

"I've already spoken to your mother superior. There's a bus leaving for Montreal in less than an hour, and they'll drive you in. Then, in Richelieu, someone will meet you at the station."

"Thank you, Father Parent. Tell Marie I'm coming right away."

● ● ●

In the bus, huddled against the window, Émilie watched the mountains roll by, the Laurentians she so loved and had thought she would never leave again. They were the ramparts protecting the Warm Welcome Hospice from the rest of the world. But, for Marie, she would walk to the ends of the earth.

Émilie had never taken the bus alone, and she was worried that she wouldn't get off at the right place. On the other hand, the anonymity of this form of transport pleased her. It reminded her of the day of her departure from Corbeil. There had been no farewell party or photographers. Later, her father had simply told the newspapers that she had not been herself in recent months and that she was going to rest in Sainte-Agathe, where the air was pure. He had not said anything about her religious vocation.

When the bus stopped at the station, Émilie rushed outside, in a hurry to get to her sister. She looked around for the person who was supposed to pick her up, but there was a large crowd and everyone seemed to be waiting for someone. Gradually, people left and others arrived, but no one came toward her. Wearily, she left the building, determined to find the convent by herself. Surely, all she had to do was ask directions.

The sidewalks were teeming with people rushing by. Either they hadn't heard of the convent, or they didn't even stop to answer Émilie's shy inquiries. She explored the nearby streets, telling herself that a convent would stand out. She had been walking for an hour, praying to God to guide her, when she suddenly realized her mistake: she was in Montreal, not Richelieu. Of course! She had to take a second bus. She had forgotten.

Completely disoriented, she couldn't retrace her steps to the bus station. Tired and soon desperate, she wandered up and down streets, holding back tears. Marie must be worried about her. As night fell, multicolored neon signs began to flash all around her, adding to her confusion. She no longer had the strength to ask directions, and she could barely put one foot in front of the other.

"Hey! You there, young lady!" Two policemen got out of a car that had pulled up beside her. "What's wrong? Where are you going?"

Finally, someone who could help her. "I'm going to see my sister at the convent of the oblates, in Richelieu."

The two uniformed men looked her over suspiciously. "What's your sister's name?" one asked.

"And what's your name?" the other added.

Maybe I shouldn't tell them, Émilie thought. If they found out that she was one of the Dionne quintuplets, the newspapers would get hold of the story, her father would hear about it, and he would be furious.

"Where do you live?"

The more they questioned her, the more Émilie withdrew into silence and the more suspicious they got. Finally, they put her in their car and took her to the police station, where they interrogated her again. When she didn't cooperate, the officer in charge said, "Since you don't have any identification, we're going to have to keep you in jail overnight."

This prospect frightened Émilie. "I'll tell you my name if you promise not to tell anyone."

The officer promised, and she told her story. When she finally told him her name, he nodded with an understanding look. "I thought your face looked familiar. One of the Dionne quints . . . wait'll I tell my wife!"

"But you promised . . ."

"That's true. I won't tell anyone."

Not knowing exactly what to do with her, the sergeant drove her to Cardinal Léger's episcopal palace. Next morning, the cardinal's chauffeur drove her back to Sainte-Agathe.

• • •

Oliva stomped into the dining room, where the family was eating breakfast. The phone call he had just received had put him in a foul mood.

"Émilie spent the night in a police station in Montreal! They picked her up on the street because she was lost."

"In jail?" Elzire cried. "What will people say?"

"And the reporters?" her husband added. "They'll make hay with this story. We should never have let her go."

Yvonne, Annette, and Cécile had stopped eating and were waiting anxiously for what would follow.

"Is she all right?" Yvonne asked.

"Making us so ashamed!" Oliva continued without bothering to answer her. "I worked my fingers to the bone for you girls, and this is how you repay me!"

Yvonne repeated her question, but her voice was drowned out by Roger's.

"Trouble, trouble," he declared. "All they've brought us is trouble. What was she doing in Montreal?"

"She was on her way to see Marie in Richelieu," Oliva said.

"Dad, is Émilie all right?" Yvonne asked anxiously. "Is she sick or anything?"

He shrugged. "She'll always be sick!" He turned to Elzire. "You go and get her before she shames us even more. Roger will drive you. And you can bring Marie back, too. They aren't ready for the outside world."

It was obvious that the prospect of this trip thrilled

neither Roger nor Elzire, but they silently went to pack their bags. Oliva returned to his office while the quints cleared the table. In the kitchen, where they could talk in private, they shared their worries about their two sisters. More than Marie's state of exhaustion and Émilie's misadventure, it was the prospect of the latter returning to Corbeil that bothered them.

"It's this house that makes Émilie sick," Annette said.

"Yes," Yvonne added. "She's much better off with the nuns in Sainte-Agathe."

Cécile nodded in agreement. Annette gave a long sigh, and said, resignedly, "But there's nothing we can do."

"I'm going to ask Mom to take me along," Cécile said firmly. "Maybe I can change her mind. She doesn't like Em, and she won't be happy to have her home."

Yvonne squeezed Cécile's arm. "Yes, Cis, do that. Netta and I will pray that it works."

Elzire let Cécile go along. The trip took place in silence, broken only by the sound of the car radio. Sitting in the back seat, Cécile went over the arguments that she would use with her mother; no doubt, the surest way to convince her would be to play on the terror that Émilie's illness instilled in her. All the newscasts on the radio were talking of the Montreal misadventure of one of the Dionne quints, casting doubt on her state of mind. Each time a report about Émilie came on, Roger's swearing punctuated the announcer's sentences, and he shot over his shoulder to Cécile, "The quints! You've been nothing but trouble since the beginning! Will it ever end?"

Cécile wisely held her tongue.

When they stopped at a snack bar along the road, the customers were talking about the affair and embellishing what they had heard on the radio.

"It doesn't surprise me," said an old man loudly, sucking on his unlit pipe. "People have always said that the Dionne quints are a bit retarded. I heard it from a good source: one of my wife's cousins worked at Dr. Dafoe's hospital."

"Maybe if they'd stayed with their family . . ." said a waitress, with an understanding look.

It made Cécile furious to hear people who knew nothing talking about her and her sisters like this.

"Hurry up and finish your coffee," she said to Roger, who was smiling sardonically.

It was only once they had arrived at the retirement home nestled in the Laurentians that Cécile had an opportunity to talk to her mother without Roger being there.

"You know, Mom, Émilie would be much better off here than at home."

Elzire stared at her daughter, wondering if this was meant to be a criticism of her. Cécile hastened to make her meaning clear.

"It's like Dad said, Émilie will always have the fits, no one can do anything, and the nuns here are used to taking care of sick people."

Cécile did not have to argue too strenuously to make her point. Finally, Elzire declared, "I will warn the nuns that she is an epileptic. If they still want to keep her anyway . . ."

While Elzire was talking with the mother superior, Cécile joined Émilie, who threw herself into her sister's arms.

"Cis! Cis, I'm so glad to see you!"

"Me too! Annette, Yvonne, and I were very worried about you."

"As you can see," Émilie replied, smiling, "I'm doing just fine."

"What happened, exactly? Did you have a seizure on the bus?"

"No. I thought I was in Richelieu when I got off the bus in Montreal. I just got lost."

Émilie told Cécile about her adventure down to the last detail. "I didn't want them to know," she concluded. "The policeman promised me he wouldn't say anything. He didn't keep his word. That wasn't very nice."

Cécile took her hand. "We came to take you home."

Émilie shivered and pulled her hand away. "There's no chance, Cis! I don't want to live anywhere else but Warm Welcome. I never want to set foot in the big house again. If you only knew how happy I am here."

"That's what I thought, Em. That's why I came with Mom. I wanted to do everything possible to make sure you don't leave with us."

Émilie smiled. "Tell me about the others, Cis. Peewee, first. I wanted so much to see her. Do you know how she is?"

"She's just exhausted, that's all. The cloister is too much for our Peewee. She's not strong enough."

"But if she has the vocation?" Émilie pleaded. "Maybe she should be in an ordinary convent, like me."

The arrival of their mother interrupted their conversation. Émilie was ready to defend her right to choose her own life, but Elzire didn't say anything about taking her home. She told them that she had warned the mother superior about her daughter's epilepsy, and the community had agreed to keep her anyway.

"We'll see what your father says," Elzire concluded. "He has the last word."

• • •

It was Lucie who opened the padlock of the gate to let the car driven by Roger into the yard. Yvonne and Annette ran outside to welcome Marie. Cécile took advantage of this to take Lucie aside and ask her, "Where's Dad?"

"In his office," Lucie answered. She shook her hand as though it had been burned, warning her sister about Oliva's terrible mood.

Cécile grabbed her sister's arm. "Émilie must not come back here. Do you understand me, Lucie?"

Lucie thought for a few seconds and then nodded. "It's best, I think. For her and for everyone."

"Talk to Dad. You're the only one who can convince him."

Lucie seemed to hesitate. She had never liked Émilie much.

Cécile insisted, looking her straight in the eyes. "Do it for me."

"Okay."

With a determined step, Lucie went to the house, passing her mother on the porch without a glance. Cécile joined her sisters and took over from Marie to answer Annette's and Yvonne's questions about Émilie.

"Come inside!" Elzire's voice was cold. "Can't you see there are cars stopped on the road?"

It was tourists, who, having bought souvenirs of the quintuplets at Mrs. Legros's store, now had the good luck to see them in the flesh — four of them, at least.

"Why don't they leave us alone?" Yvonne muttered as the sisters hastened inside. She thought nostalgically about her month in Montreal. Walking without fear of being recognized, taking the bus without drawing looks,

188

and being a person like others, one among many, had led to a luxurious feeling of freedom. When would she have it again? Oh, to stop being a quintuplet in the eyes of the world, no longer to be one except in her heart. If only being a quint were a secret that one carried inside oneself . . . *It's an impossible dream*, she told herself.

Coming home to Quintland, down this country road where millions of visitors had flocked, was for Yvonne like shrugging on her old "quintuplet" costume. Everything around her was a monument to the celebrity that she would happily have gone without. The old house where the miracle took place, the hospital where so many films were shot, the observation gallery where the curious could watch five little girls play, the three souvenir shops, the parking lot, the public toilets . . . then this big house where the Dionne family reunion had taken place! And everywhere, the high fences topped with barbed wire.

Here, Yvonne could never forget that she was one of the "famous" quintuplets. She had so many memories — happy ones from a very distant past, and other ones that were more recent and much more painful — that she felt as though she had already lived a very long time. Oh, if only she could forget!

When I leave here again, she told herself as she crossed the threshold, *I'll never come back.*

• • •

Lucie had convinced her father to let Émilie stay in the convent, and Elzire had concluded, without realizing that she was taking up Cécile's own argument, "The nuns are used to taking care of sick people. Émilie is in the right place."

Cécile, Annette, Yvonne, and Marie spent the summer

189

in the big brick house under the watchful eye of their mother. It was as if they had gone back in time. But there had been a change in all of them, fragile though it was: they had had a taste of independence and liberty, and they could no longer ignore it. Day after day, each led a silent battle against the old habits of submissiveness and dependence that threatened to take over, against the feelings of guilt that were no less strong for being baseless.

Behind these feelings was their father's attempt to turn back the clock to the time when they had lived under his thumb. Then there were their mother's tears, complaints, and recriminations. And there was the rest of the family trying to convince them that they were good for nothing, accusing them of having made their parents unhappy and ruining their father's health.

Another thing that hadn't changed was the endless round of chores to be done. As they worked in the garden one day, Annette suddenly said, "Don't look up. Keep working and talking. Someone is watching at the window."

She changed rows to get closer to her sisters. They were weeding, moving from row to row at the same speed so that they could talk to each other. Opportunities for the four of them to be alone together were so few and far between!

"Don't tire yourself out, Peewee," Yvonne recommended. "Just look as if you're doing something."

They did this chore in the cool of the morning, since the afternoons had been scorching this summer. Now that August had come, the question of their immediate future was even more pressing. When they had an opportunity to talk together, the conversation quickly turned to this topic.

Marie was talking about going back to the convent in Quebec City, and her sisters were doing their best to convince her that life in the cloister was too difficult for her.

"Give yourself some time, a few months, to see things more clearly," Cécile suggested.

"Yes, take a year if you need to," added Yvonne, picking a bean and eating it.

"What would I do?" Marie asked. "I don't want to stay here."

"Of course not," Annette declared. "I don't know yet what I'm going to do, Peewee, but I'm sure I'm leaving. If I have to, I'll go back to Nicolet."

"And where are Mom and Dad in all of this?" Cécile asked. "We aren't children any more, but they can't see that."

Cécile had wanted to start nursing school this autumn, but she knew that her parents would probably dismiss it out of hand. Yvonne, who had made the same choice as Cécile, also worried about her parents' reaction. The fear that had been in the back of her mind when she had come home at the end of June had only grown since.

"Time to make dinner!"

Hearing their mother's order shouted at the top of her lungs, the quints stood up in perfect unison. Seeing how quickly they had all reacted, Annette muttered, "We're not out of the woods yet!"

That afternoon, the ambiance in the dining room was strange. Oliva did not come to eat at the table. He stayed in his office, where he had spent the entire morning on the telephone. Elzire was restless. She stood up and wandered in and out, her expression worried and annoyed by turns. The radio was playing catchy tunes that lightened the atmosphere, and Roger and Serge, who were eating with the quints, were in a good mood. There were fresh blueberries for dessert, and the pot of cream was making its way around the table when the phone rang.

"The telephone again!" Serge exclaimed.

A few minutes later, Elzire burst into the room, her face white.

"Stay calm, little girls. Émilie is dead."

8

"Cécile, you will never feel so bad again in your whole life."

As she said this to herself, Cécile dug her nails into the palms of her clenched fists. She, Marie, Annette, and Yvonne were watching through the window of their mother's bedroom as the black hearse came into the yard bearing a most precious treasure. Reporters and onlookers stood on the other side of the fence, many of them making the sign of the cross or dabbing at their eyes.

Cécile's nails bit into the tender skin of her hands, but she didn't notice, for the pain in her heart overwhelmed any other. Her grief was burned into her flesh. The loss of Émilie was like a physical wound. A part of each of the surviving quints was laid out in the coffin in the hearse. None of them would ever be the same again; a part of each had died.

When the coffin, carried by four men, disappeared from view, the quints turned away from the window and caught each other's eye, not saying a word. They had not yet found the words to express their anguish. All they could do was look at each other — four ashen, drawn faces, each a living mirror of the death mask of the others — then burst into tears and sob in each other's arms. Sometimes they stared at the wall, numb, unaware of the hours passing by, tormented by images that tore at their hearts. They could think of nothing but a face that was already no more than a memory, of withdrawing into a shell that contained only pure pain.

When their mother had announced Émilie's death, the world had stopped turning. For several minutes, they had been in a daze as Elzire's words slowly sank in. It was impossible! How could one of them die without the others? How could they be living if Émilie's heart had stopped beating? Their world was crumbling around them. Roger had stood up and turned off the radio. Silence had fallen like a leaden shroud. *"Émilie is dead."* The words had worked their poison into the hearts of the surviving quints. First, the horror had hit, then the searing pain. They had run to their rooms and thrown themselves on their beds, incapable of anything but tears.

Thirty hours had passed since then, but it could have been thirty days or thirty minutes. Sorrow had obliterated time. None of them had been able to find the words to console her grief-stricken sisters. Did words exist? Their faith in God told them that they would be with Émilie again one day, but between now and then, how would they find the strength to live?

Annette found no comfort in her mechanically recited prayers. For her, mourning turned quickly to rebellion. Their birth was supposed to be a miracle — so why let them survive, only to kill them all at twenty years of age by stealing one of them away?

In the neighboring bed, Cécile cried endless tears. She refused to believe what she'd been told. The alarm clock would ring and she would open her eyes, relieved to discover that she was awakening from an atrocious nightmare. She would be in the room that she shared with Émilie at the Family Institute in Nicolet, and Émilie would be asleep, her smiling angel's face on the pillow. But no, she wasn't dreaming. Such pain could never have been dreamt up.

Curled up on her side, Yvonne stared at the empty bed beside her own. She had no more tears to shed, but she found it hard to breathe, as though her chest were in a vise. The room was still full of Émilie's things. It still vibrated with her laughter. Yvonne blamed herself for not having been there to protect her sister just one more time, to keep her alive, to stave off her death. Something had been extinguished inside Yvonne, a flame that would never again be revived.

Marie lived through her pain like a caterpillar in its cocoon, not noticing when Lucie entered or left their bedroom. Nothing existed outside her, and little subsisted within her, only a scream that she could not get out. Death was faceless; if she were to unveil it, it could as easily have worn her own face as Émilie's. It was she, the smallest one, the last born, who should have died, not Émilie. She would have given anything to be laid out instead of her sister, or at least beside her.

• • •

"Let's go," Yvonne murmured to the three others.

In silence, they went downstairs to welcome their sister into the house one last time. Even though they wanted to see her face and touch her cheek once more, they knew that the sight of her in her varnished wooden casket would be excruciating.

The coffin had been set by the windows in the big living room, on the left as they went in. Funeral-parlor employees had placed prie-dieux in front of the open coffin. Their legs trembling, the surviving quints moved forward to see Émilie. Marie felt faint and held onto Yvonne's arm. Cécile bit her lips so that she wouldn't cry out, and Annette clasped her hands together to control their trembling.

Émilie, in a blue dress (the color she had liked best when they lived in The Dafoe Hospital and Nursery), was resting in a fluffy bed of white satin. A white crucifix and a rosary had been placed in her hands. To cover the pallor of death, thick make-up had been applied to her face. It looked so strange — she'd never worn make-up when she was alive!

Weeping, the four sisters approached. One by one, they touched Émilie's cheek, held her cold hands, and kissed her on the forehead. Afterward, they remained close to the coffin, looking at the remains of their sister with an unceasing incredulity. This body was *their* body! Created from the same egg! How could one part of a being die without the rest dying?

Moved by the quintuplets' sorrow, the funeral-home employees finished arranging the flowers around the coffin as discreetly as possible. But Marie, Annette, Cécile, and Yvonne were indifferent to what was going on around them. Weeping silently, they had one last silent conversation with Émilie, while behind them the rest of the family responded aloud to Elzire Dionne's recited prayers and invocations.

After half an hour, Marie began to feel tired and knelt

on the Persian rug. The three others quickly knelt with her. Together, they recited Hail Marys, casting despairing glances at their sister's closed eyelids. Not wanting to drown out the quints' thin thread of prayer, the other people in the living room did not join in.

The quints sat with Émilie until their mother sent them into their bedrooms for the night. But none of them could sleep, and they returned to the living room as soon as the sky was light. The house slowly woke up around them. It was the arrival of Mr. Sasse, the photographer, that finally broke the spell. Cécile did not want pictures to be taken, but Sasse reminded them that they were bound by contract.

"Just one, then," Cécile finally conceded.

The four young women, with the obedience born of years of training, gathered around the coffin to strike the pose he asked for. The photographer took the ultimate picture of the Dionne quintuplets: the very last time they would all be together.

Émilie is still playing the part of a quintuplet for the camera, Yvonne thought bitterly, *even though she's dead*.

More people arrived, more flowers were delivered.

"She was an angel, the soul of innocence," Oliva declared to the people around him.

And you profited well from it! was Cécile's silent retort.

When the photograph had been taken, the quints went back to their rooms so that they wouldn't have to hear the condolences, even the sincere ones, of the other mourners.

Hundreds of people had come, and they formed a long line along the fence of the compound. There were neighbors and friends in dark suits and black dresses, tourists in light and colorful clothes — some simply satisfying their curiosity, others deeply moved — and a horde of reporters. Cars were parked on either side of the road as far as the eye could see. It looked like the heyday of Quintland, except that this procession was heading not toward The Dafoe Hospital and Nursery but in the opposite direction, toward the door of the big house built by the father of the quintuplets. The previous evening, Oliva had sent dozens of telegrams inviting people to the funeral. For the first time since the big house was built, eleven years earlier, he unlocked the gate and opened his doors to all comers. Sitting in an armchair to the right of her daughter's coffin, Elzire welcomed visitors with dignity. More than five thousand people walked by Émilie's coffin that Sunday.

When he leaned toward Elzire, it was not condolences that Father Sauvé offered her. Sternly, he said, "You are partly responsible for her death, Mrs. Dionne."

She sat stock-still, but her eyes moved insistently toward the door. The priest knew that his frankness meant he would no longer be welcome in this house, but he owed it to the dead young woman to say something.

News of Émilie's death had been spread by the doctor who signed her death certificate. The newspapers devoted special editions to the story, and it was the top item on the radio broadcasts. People were stunned to learn that Émilie had been suffering from epilepsy since moving into her parents' home and that the Dionne family had been able to keep this secret for so long. Émilie's death was reported down to the last detail, and many of those who had once traveled to Quintland to catch a glimpse of five carefree girls truly mourned.

The day before she died, Émilie had been at a picnic for the dozen pensioners at the Warm Welcome Hospice.

198

She had had an epileptic seizure and had hurt her ankle as she fell. Thinking she might have another seizure, she had asked for a nun to stay in her room to watch over her. During the night, she had had three more seizures; in the morning, she had stayed in bed, refusing to eat, and had gone back to sleep. Since she was resting peacefully, the nun keeping watch over her had gone off to mass with the rest of the community. Upon their return from the chapel, the nuns had found Émilie lifeless. The coroner who performed the autopsy explained that Émilie had not died of epilepsy. After a final seizure, she had rolled over on her stomach and had suffocated with her face in her pillow. It was an accidental death.

This was the hardest thing of all for the quints to bear. Émilie's death had not been inevitable. All it would have taken was someone at her bedside, a pair of arms to turn her onto her back. They would never have left their sister alone under such circumstances. They would have known what to do. But the nuns hadn't realized how serious Émilie's illness was. No doubt, they hadn't been well informed . . .

On the following Monday morning, Cécile, Marie, Annette, and Yvonne bade heart-wrenching farewells to Émilie before the coffin was closed. Under a dark, threatening sky, the funeral procession made its way to the small red-brick church in Corbeil, built in the prosperous times when five identical little girls had attracted millions of visitors and made the region rich. This morning, it was as if those times had returned: cars were bumper to bumper in the roads around Corbeil and there were many more people than the parish church could hold.

The quints hardly noticed the crowd or recognized the people who had played a role in their life. Each was wrapped within a cloak of melancholy; they still had to come to terms with the fact that they would never see Émilie again. They were everything to one another; losing their sister made them feel like widows and orphans at the same time. They would have to learn how to live all over again as only four.

The funeral service, attended by twenty priests, was presided over by Fathers La France, Sauvé, and Bélanger. Cécile found the black-draped church gloomy. Everything was so dark, so sad, and the ceremony was endless! When she thought about the burial, her last shred of strength evaporated. Going to the cemetery would be senseless, for Cécile was trying to keep Émilie alive within her soul. She grabbed Annette's hand and squeezed it very hard, and Marie leaned her shoulder against Yvonne's. They needed to be in physical contact, to feel that they were still part of a single living body, to believe that Émilie would always be with them, not in the coffin at the foot of the altar.

The grave, which their brother Armand had helped to dig, was located beside the two gray crosses that marked their grandparents' graves. The only bit of color in the monochrome landscape was provided by a mountain of flowers bordering the open hole. The crowd was so thick that it completely blocked off the other gravestones and monuments.

The quints followed Father La France and the children of the choir, who were carrying a large crucifix and candles. Flashbulbs momentarily lit up their wan faces. It all seemed so unreal; it was as though the ceremony had nothing to do with them, as though it was happening to someone else. Émilie was still with them, an invisible but palpable presence.

A drenching rain began to fall.

The quintuplets' grief lost its sharp sting. They measured time dating from their sister's death — three days, then four, then a week — waiting for the mourning to become less painful. But Émilie never died in her sisters' hearts; on the contrary, she remained as present within them as when she had been alive.

The rest of the family, however, buried Émilie's memory much more quickly. Her death had shocked and saddened them, but, once the funeral that had brought them together was over, they returned to daily life, with its usual tensions and quarrels, as if nothing had happened. The coffin was barely in the ground when Elzire began getting rid of her dead daughter's personal possessions. The children who lived far from Corbeil left with their share of the booty — coats, dresses, or shoes.

The quints also received souvenirs of Émilie: her old slippers, her prayer book, and some trinkets. Yet again, they were being treated differently from their sisters, but they didn't care. What they really wanted — a word of comfort from their mother — was not forthcoming. All that Elzire said to Yvonne was, "It's a good thing she didn't die here. There would have been an inquiry." And, to Cécile, "I think Émilie didn't love me." Cécile didn't answer — no matter what she said, it could only make things worse.

Along with the pain of Émilie's loss, the question of their immediate future occupied all of Yvonne's, Annette's, Marie's, and Cécile's thoughts. Their parents wanted them to stay at home, or else to return to the Family Institute in Nicolet, but the quints had other plans, and this time they defended them. They were emboldened by the example

Émilie had set for them by refusing to come home and instead returning to her convent in Sainte-Agathe.

Cécile and Yvonne were still resolved to go to nursing school, even though Elzire continued to express her objections to any profession in the medical field. They came out of these interminable discussions with their mother more determined than ever to follow their own paths, manifesting a spirit of independence that surprised even them.

Since there was no longer any question of the four young women living away from each other, Marie and Annette registered at Collège Marguerite-Bourgeoys, in Westmount, not far from the Côte-Vertu hospital where their sisters would be studying. Tired of fighting, Oliva and Elzire Dionne had grudgingly consented to let them go. But after the decision was made, the atmosphere in the house deteriorated even further. The ambivalence that the others had always felt toward the "little girls" turned into a dull hate, perceptible in their looks and words, and even more in their silences. For no reason that the quints could fathom, Lucie ignored them completely for the rest of the summer.

Elzire's goodbye was cold. From the porch, she watched her quints climb into Oliva's Cadillac. Both mother and daughters were aware that an era was coming to an end. Elzire felt that she had failed, and she was intensely bitter. *Those ingrates!* she thought. September 6, 1954, was a date she would never forget!

As the car turned onto the road, the quints glanced back one more time at the big brick house so full of their tears and despair. Though they would come back to visit their parents, they knew that they would never again live there. In nine months, they would be adults, and no one would have legal authority over them.

Out of the corner of her eye, Annette saw the abandoned buildings: the house where they had been born, the hospital that had become their private elementary school and boarding school, the observation gallery where the whispering wind had now replaced the visitors' murmurs, the sentry post, and the fences, now absurd in their uselessness. *The cage is open*, she thought, *and the birds are flying away.*

The image of a short man, his too-small hat perched on his head, suddenly popped into her mind. He got out of his car, which was gray with dust, climbed the front steps of the hospital, and approached the five identical little girls, whom he had never managed to tell apart. Pipe in mouth, he smiled widely under his salt-and-pepper mustache. The large camera on a tripod clicked, Dr. Dafoe opened his arms, and a nurse murmured, "Go see the doctor. Go on." Annette and her sisters ran toward the man in the rumpled suit. *Did we love him*, she wondered, *or were we just making believe for the photographer?* She didn't know. But today, finally breaking free of her birthplace, she had warm thoughts for the old doctor. At least he had always respected them and treated them fairly.

From the top of the hill, Annette could see all of Quintland, a kingdom that had never really been more than a hayfield, a theater in which she and her sisters had acted out a backwards fairy tale, playing first princesses and then Cinderellas. But it was time to stop play-acting; real life was beginning today. Annette looked at her sisters' faces. They looked as tense as she knew her own must be. Cécile gave her a slight smile that seemed to say, *I know what you're feeling — anguish and relief mixed together.*

Oliva drove to North Bay in silence, his face inscrutable.

He, too, realized that the quints were leaving forever, and this could very soon make life complicated . . .

Suitcases at their feet, the quints stood in a group on the platform waiting for the train. Annette, Cécile, and Yvonne surrounded Marie; they felt the need to protect her, since she was still very shaken by Émilie's death. The idea of living in a large city frightened her, and she was not certain that her health would allow her to study at college, but she would not be separated from her sisters for anything in the world.

A few steps away, Oliva was talking to a railway employee and keeping a discreet eye on his "little girls." They were not ready to fly with their own wings, but to keep them at home against their will risked starting a controversy in the newspapers. He would rather tell reporters that they had gone reluctantly, resigning themselves to leaving home only because there was no other way to continue their education.

Trying to ignore the dozens of pairs of eyes staring at them, the quints stared out at Lake Nipissing, sparkling beyond the freight-train switching yard. Since Émilie's funeral, they had regarded the crowds and reporters as an intrusion. The curiosity that had always surrounded them had become intolerable; more and more, they wanted privacy and anonymity, and to have nothing to do with the roles that had been imposed upon them.

A loud, jangling bell announced the train's entry into the station.

"All right," Oliva said flatly, "goodbye."

"Goodbye," they answered. "We'll see you at Christmas."

"That's right."

"We'll keep writing every week," Annette added, to appease him.

Her father nodded, then spun on his heel and returned to his car without waiting for the train to leave the station. This was his final gesture of disapproval; he had stopped trying to change their minds two weeks before.

The quints were happy that he'd gone quickly; he might have tried a last-minute trick to keep them from leaving. Nevertheless they didn't breathe easy until the train began moving.

"Ohh!" Yvonne let out a loud sigh of relief.

"I feel a bit ashamed . . ." Annette admitted, sheepishly.

"That you don't feel sad to be leaving them?" Cécile asked, bluntly. "That you're happy to go? Don't you think all five of us have paid a hundred times over for the right to be happy?"

There it was! Cécile had simply said out loud what they had all been thinking since that morning, when they had attended a mass celebrated in Émilie's memory: they were leaving without her. Their sister wasn't with them on this big day. She would never again be with them. The rhythm of metal wheels on rail ties became deafening as the silence suddenly grew deeper. The four young women exchanged bereft looks, and Yvonne pulled a sobbing Marie to her.

"It's been a month already," murmured Cécile, unable to hold back her tears.

"It hurts just as much as the first day," Annette whispered.

Yvonne bit her lips and wept silently. For fifteen minutes, they simply held hands or touched each other's arm or shoulder, so that they wouldn't feel alone.

Cécile and Yvonne were the first to get ahold of themselves. Because they had decided what to do with their lives, they had the most to gain from leaving Corbeil. Lately, they had found some willpower, learned to express themselves more freely, and let themselves be bossed around less often.

It was more difficult for Marie and Annette to leave the family home, because they were less certain what they wanted to do next. Annette had chosen music, and Marie literature, simply because they liked those subjects, without knowing where it would lead them.

When she finally sat up and leaned back in her seat to dry her eyes, Marie murmured, "Montreal scares me a little." She couldn't help thinking of the time Émilie got lost there. "What's it like?" she asked.

"Well, I don't know the city that well," Yvonne said. "I didn't go off campus very much." She tried to come up with a more positive response. "It's lively, especially St. Catherine Street, near Eaton's and Morgan's. It's full of stores, movie theaters, and restaurants. Where Marguerite-Bourgeoys is, in Westmount, it's quiet and there are lots of trees. The college is halfway up the mountain, and you can see the tops of trees, and the houses nestled among them, and it looks like a big forest. The best thing is that you can walk around, take the bus, shop, without people recognizing you. You can talk to people without having them feel self-conscious or shy — they don't stare at you as if you were an invalid."

The others cheered up and began to chat about the big city where the unknown awaited. There would be so much to discover, so many new people to meet. It would be a bit like starting their life all over again — or, maybe, learning about life for the first time.

• • •

Yvonne and Cécile shared a room at the student nurses' residence behind the Notre Dame de l'Espérance

206

Hospital. It was an old building in a quiet suburb, sprinkled with vacant lots and still bordered with farms. Inside the hospital, however, life was exciting.

Their days were very full, since, in addition to tending the sick and studying nursing, they had to catch up on certain basic subjects like chemistry and philosophy. They didn't complain, since it was exactly the life they had expected. As time went by, they discovered the deeper motivation for their choice: by devoting themselves to the infirm, they were able to lose themselves in others, and be closer to God.

The slight odor of antiseptic and disinfectant that always floated in the corridors of the hospital became, for them, the very scent of liberty. Here, they had a privacy that had been unimaginable before. Their room had a lock on the door; nobody read their mail or got upset if they spoke privately; when they didn't have homework, they could go out and do what they liked.

In Nicolet, they had been forbidden to wear make-up, but here they were encouraged to wear lipstick to raise the patients' morale. The innocuous gesture of putting on lipstick every morning became symbolic of both their hard-won freedom and their femininity. As well, the hospital offered innumerable possibilities for friendship and camaraderie, things that had become important since they had discovered them at Villa Notre-Dame. Painfully shy at first, they quickly began to feel at ease in daily contact with the other students with whom they shared classes and often difficult work. Affinities were found, partnerships developed, and friendships born.

Collège Marguerite-Bourgeoys offered Marie and Annette an environment as diversified and passionate as that in which Cécile and Yvonne were immersed at the hospital. None of the sisters would have hesitated to say they were happy, although Marie was still affected by Émilie's death. An inexplicable weariness and undefined anxiety formed a screen between her and the world, preventing her from enjoying her new life.

Though each sister had another nearby, they missed being all together. Being apart for more than a day had always been difficult for them — feelings of solitude soon shaded into sadness, and they absolutely had to make contact, at least by telephone or letter. It was the sort of pull, like the magnetism between lovers, that varied depending on distance and circumstances. Now that there were only four of them, the need to see each other was even greater.

Therefore there was much traveling back and forth between the college and the hospital. The distance was only four miles, but it involved changing buses twice, which made the trip interminably long. Not used to public transit, the quints preferred to take taxis. This seriously depleted the pocket money that their father supplied, and they had to economize on other expenses. But the need to see each other was more pressing than any other.

Although strolling through the quiet neighborhoods around the college and the hospital presented no problems, going downtown was a different matter. For their first outing to the department stores on St. Catherine Street, the quints went together, wearing sunglasses as a disguise. But it didn't work! In Eaton's, a curious crowd gathered and followed them wherever they went, as though they were movie stars. This curiosity, as innocent or friendly as it may have been, terrorized them, and they fled. The same thing happened wherever they went, so they headed home, bitterly disappointed. The anonymity of the large city was being denied them. After this trying experience, they went downtown only in pairs or singly with friends.

• • •

Sitting in a booth at the back of a coffee shop, Yvonne and Cécile looked at each other, disappointed.

"I can't wear this!" Cécile exclaimed, holding up the black dress that she had just bought.

Yvonne shook her head, discouraged. She wasn't happy with her purchases, either. "It doesn't seem right, Cis. We're dumber than country bumpkins. We're twenty years old, and we don't even know how to buy a pair of stockings!"

"We don't know anything," Cécile said resentfully.

All four quints knew that they had not been properly prepared to face life in the real world, even with regard to the most basic daily activity. It had been deemed not a good thing for them to learn. How to behave in a store, choose clothing, and compare prices seemed to pose insoluble problems. They had no idea of the value of money, what sizes they wore, or the cuts and colors that would look best on them.

How could their classmates think going shopping was fun? For Marie, Annette, Yvonne, and Cécile, it was simply a necessary evil. They sneaked into a department store, bought the first dress they saw, and rushed out, red-faced with embarrassment. They ended up with clothes just like those their mother used to buy for them: dark colors and much too big. This situation only confirmed their opinion that they were incapable of making decisions for themselves, or of doing anything without asking permission.

"Things will change," Cécile said decidedly, sliding her shopping bag under her seat.

"What can we expect? They always kept us dependent, and they stifled any sense of initiative we might have had."

"We have to do something, Ivy. I've decided to learn how to get along in life. It may take time, but I'll do it."

"Me, too," Yvonne answered, encouraged by her sister's determination, which seemed to grow from day to day. "But Netta? And especially Peewee?"

"If we help them and support them . . ."

"Hush! They're coming."

Annette and Marie were walking quickly, their eyes down so that they wouldn't see the faces turning toward them. The restaurant customers had noticed that the two young women who had come in bore a strange resemblance to the two sitting in the booth, and they drew the obvious conclusion: the Dionne quintuplets! The newspapers had mentioned that they were now living in Montreal.

Annette and Marie kissed their sisters and sat down.

"How was the film?"

Instead of answering Yvonne's question, Annette threw a folded newspaper onto the table.

"Have you read this?" she asked, with a mixture of surprise and anger.

"What does it say?" Cécile asked.

"It's about us!" Marie said. "Yet again!"

Yvonne shrugged. "All we have to do is not read those articles and we won't get hurt."

"But other people read them," Cécile said. "Oh, if only they would just forget about us."

Marie unfolded her copy of *La Patrie* and pushed it toward Yvonne. "Read this."

210

Her curiosity piqued, Yvonne glanced quickly at the article, then started to read aloud, in a voice just loud enough for her sisters to hear. The paper said that Émilie's share of the quintuplets' fund was $171,035.

"How much?" Cécile asked, incredulous.

Yvonne checked the figure and repeated it. The article went on to say that Émilie's inheritance would be divided equally between Oliva, Elzire, and their twelve children.

"My God!" Cécile exclaimed. "That's lots of money!"

"What is the quintuplets' fund?" Yvonne asked.

"Keep reading," Annette told her. "You'll see."

The article stated that each of them would get an equal share of Émilie's inheritance, which had been her part of the income earned by the quintuplets when, as children, they had appeared in films and advertising campaigns. Their father was managing the fund under the supervision of the government of Ontario.

Yvonne stopped reading and looked up at her sisters. They were as amazed as she was. No one had ever told them that they had their own money. They had always believed that everything they were given came out of their father's pocket, and they'd felt guilty for costing him so much. If they ever wanted a piece of costume jewelry or hair ribbons, their mother always complained that they had extravagant taste.

"That would explain lots of things," Annette murmured.

Her sisters nodded. Yes, this shone a new light on the remarks and allusions that family members and visitors had made in the past, words that had always been incomprehensible to them. The comment by the principal of the Family Institute — "You're rich enough to buy the whole school!" — suddenly made sense. At the time, they'd thought that the "you" referred to the family of a rich man, Oliva Dionne. If they had their own money, it would go a long way toward explaining the way their family treated them. But why had such a mystery been made of it? Why had they never been told?

"Somehow," Yvonne said pensively, "in the back of my mind I always knew it."

"In any case, it proves that money doesn't bring happiness," Annette retorted. "I was never so unhappy as I was in the big house!"

"There's still lots of time left to suffer," Marie said, with a teasing smile.

"Nothing will ever be worse than that. I only wish I could be as happy as I was in our hospital."

Marie shook her head. "That's impossible. Remember, back then, we thought we were related to the princesses of England!"

They all smiled, except for Cécile, who was lost in thought. "A hundred and seventy-one thousand," she murmured, distractedly. "That sounds like a lot of money."

For Cécile and her sisters, who had never had more than a few dollars in their pockets, the size of the fortune that they were said to possess meant nothing. What could one buy with it? A car, or only a bicycle? Would it pay for a fur coat? Aside from the cost of a taxi ride, a meal at a restaurant, or a pair of nylon stockings — in short, anything that could be bought with a few dollars — they didn't have the slightest idea of the value of things.

Annette had an image of herself at five years old, playing grocery store with her sisters. She and Marie were at the counter, and the three others were customers. They had a pretend cash register and money but real jars of jam, and the big black camera was clicking away on its tripod. Annette shivered involuntarily: she had never set

212

foot in a real grocery store! Now that school was over, she would have to learn how to cook, which meant going to the market. Suddenly, she felt completely helpless.

"What should we do?" Marie asked.

"We'll wait until they talk to us about it," Cécile answered, glancing at the others. "That would avoid lots of trouble . . ."

They were still scared of their parents. Their independence, even a semblance of independence, was still partly a dream. They dutifully wrote their parents every week, even if they had nothing new to report and more to keep back than to say.

• • •

Sitting by the telephone, Cécile looked, perplexed, at the number scribbled on a scrap of paper. She had no idea whose it was. A colleague had taken the message while she was in class. No doubt, it was a friend from Villa Notre-Dame or from Nicolet who was passing through Montreal. She dialed the number, and a male voice answered. After hesitating a couple of seconds, she explained, "Somebody told me to call this number. My name is Cécile Dionne."

"Oh! Hello, Miss Dionne. My name is Laurent Bouchard. I'm the one who called you."

He paused, but Cécile was too mystified to say anything, so he continued, "I heard you and your sisters are being held captive in Montreal."

"That's absolutely false!" Cécile cried.

"I read it in the papers."

"Reporters say whatever they like!" she answered, ready to hang up.

He laughed heartily. "I should know that, since I work at Radio-Canada."

A reporter! She should have known.

"I don't give interviews, Mr. . . ."

"Bouchard. But I'm not a reporter, I'm a technician."

Now, she was completely confused.

"So, you're not a prisoner! I'm glad. Cécile . . . you don't mind if I call you by your first name? My sister's name is Cécile, too."

"If you like," she replied skeptically. "As for our situation, you should know that we are free to come and go like the other students."

"Oh," he said, sounding disappointed. "And I had hoped to come to your rescue, even though I don't have a white horse or a suit of armor."

She couldn't help laughing.

"If you're free, Cécile, would you have coffee with me? I'd like to chat face to face."

The invitation took her by surprise, and she was silent for a moment.

"You have nothing to fear," he insisted. "I am a gentleman."

His voice was soft and warm. *A coffee won't commit me to anything,* she thought. *And won't it prove I'm an independent woman?*

"A coffee? I accept."

The moment she hung up, Cécile regretted her decision. She knew nothing about him, and all he knew about her was what he'd read in the papers. But it was too late to back out. Oh well, she could drink a cup of coffee in five minutes.

The night before their date, Cécile had trouble sleeping. She was sorry that she had gotten herself involved in

214

this and didn't dare tell anyone about it, certain that they would think she was out of her mind. What would she find to say to someone she didn't know? How did one behave alone with a man? She could always stand him up — but that would be an act of cowardice unworthy of her newfound freedom.

Laurent was waiting at the hospital entrance at the appointed time. He offered her a red carnation, then shook her hand. Tall and thin, he had sparkling eyes and an attractive smile. They strolled down the peaceful, deserted streets of Côte Saint-Luc, then went into a restaurant and sat down. Cécile felt awkward, and she stammered with shyness. But Laurent talked enough for both of them. He had an unshakable confidence in life and in himself, and Cécile envied his enthusiasm. Everything seemed so easy for him! She, on the other hand, always had doubts, was never satisfied with the results of her exams, and worried that she wasn't devoted enough to the sick people she cared for. Hearing him talk made her forget her own limitations for a moment.

Before saying goodbye in front of the hospital, Laurent said, "I'd like to see you again, Cécile. Do you like movies?"

"I love them."

"Me too. When's your next day off?"

Everything was going too fast. She wanted time to think, but he was waiting for her answer, his eyes full of hope. He took her hand.

"Next Thursday," she answered, withdrawing her hand.

The die was cast. Cécile went to her room, still incredulous. That someone could be interested in her, as a woman and not as one of the Dionne quintuplets, was overwhelming. This date made her nervous. In Corbeil, she had been taught that love and sex were sins, except within marriage, and the nuns in Nicolet had not contradicted this idea. The quints had always been led to believe that marriage was not for them, that their fate was to spend the rest of their lives in the family home, or to become nuns. And above all, men were not to be trusted. But as the day of her date with Laurent approached, Cécile realized that she was looking forward to seeing him again.

When she told her sisters about meeting him for coffee, they couldn't believe their ears.

"What's this?!" Yvonne exclaimed. "You went to a restaurant with someone you don't know who called you on the telephone?"

"He held your hand!" Annette said, awed.

"He just shook my hand, to say hello," Cécile protested.

She glanced at Marie, expecting her to tease her yet again about the boy from Minnesota who had held her hand when she was seventeen. But Marie just smiled a sheepish and ambivalent grin and asked her sister to describe her new friend, which Cécile did with relish.

"What did he say?" Yvonne asked. "Tell us absolutely everything."

Marie, Annette, and Yvonne listened raptly to Cécile's report. They were amazed that such a thing could happen to one of them. Might they be able to lead a normal life, after all? To judge by Cécile's enchanted smile and the joy that lit up her face, she was in love. She denied it, but her sisters were not fooled; after all, they knew her as well as they knew themselves.

"Are you going to introduce us to him?" Yvonne asked.

"It's a bit soon. Listen, I've only seen him once."

"But the next time, you'll be in a dark movie theater!" Annette teased, with a wink. Cécile blushed.

Marie touched her arm. "We're very happy for you, Cis," she said in a serious voice.

Yvonne added, "If you were brave enough to go out with a man, maybe the rest of us can take charge of our lives, too."

Cécile was suddenly anxious about the importance that her sisters were placing on her date. It was as if they were charging her with a mission.

"They mustn't hear about this at home!" she said. Their father hadn't wanted them even to have girlfriends; what would he do when he knew a man had entered the picture?

• • •

Cécile's second date was followed by many others, and her idyll with Laurent made her sisters dream about romance. Despite their mother's tirades against men, they all hoped that someday they would meet gentle, good, and educated men, whose very existence would transform the world into a more hospitable place. Unconsciously, each had an immense need to love and be loved and was ready to latch onto the first man who showed an interest in her.

Although Marie was happy for Cécile, love was the least of her concerns just then. Since Émilie's death, she no longer felt the joy in living that had once overflowed in her. While her sisters were slowly blossoming in the real world, she remained taciturn and withdrawn, and nothing seemed to be able to lift her out of her depression.

At the end of October, Marie went to Corbeil for the weekend, and her parents pressured her to stay home. Elzire complained that she'd been abandoned, that she felt terribly lonely without her quintuplets and, finally, in tears, begged Marie to stay. The sensitive, devoted young

217

woman did not have the heart to return to Montreal as she had planned.

Once they got over the shock, Annette, Yvonne, and Cécile were very disappointed. Their father quickly issued a statement saying that Marie wasn't happy in the city and that he and his wife were very pleased to have one of the quintuplets at home. Marie, he said, was finding contentment helping her mother. But her sisters, back in Montreal, were far from convinced. They knew that Marie had fallen back into the old rut of total submission to their parents' desires. As well as being sad for their sister, they worried for themselves. Perhaps it was not as easy as they had imagined to liberate themselves from old, ingrained habits, to throw off the shackles of their dependency. Were they as strong as they thought?

9

"I know why they made us come home," Yvonne murmured.

Cécile and Annette, who had been staring out at the countryside through the train window, turned to look at her.

Their mother had been planning to bring Marie to Montreal to celebrate their twenty-first birthday, but at the last minute, their father had asked them to come to Corbeil instead. They didn't like the idea, but how could they say no to their father?

"What do you mean?" Cécile asked.

Yvonne showed Cécile a week-old copy of the *Nugget* that she had found under her seat.

"Read it aloud," Cécile said, and Annette nodded.

Instead, Yvonne folded the newspaper and summed up what she had read. "It says the quintuplets will have about $800,000 when they turn twenty-one. Dad explains that we will place this sum in a trust and that a lawyer, Mr. Donnely, has prepared the necessary papers. It also says that coming into all this money won't change our lives a bit."

This was the first they had heard of such a thing.

"More secrets!" Annette said indignantly.

"It's always been like this," Cécile replied wearily. "Why would it change now?"

Yvonne sighed in despair. She always dreaded visiting the big house, knowing that she and her sisters would have to bear their parents' recriminations and complaints. Now, with this matter of the trust, the atmosphere might be completely unbearable. Only the overwhelming desire to see Marie gave her the strength to keep going and not take the train straight back to Montreal once she arrived in North Bay. Poor Marie . . . The tone of her letters, uninformative and guarded, led them to believe that she had fallen back under their parents' yoke.

"What are we going to do?" Annette asked.

"We have to read everything carefully before we sign," Cécile answered, with the mistrust of her parents that nine years of living with them had taught her. The train was going too fast for her taste . . . Soon, she would be surrounded once again by the hate in the big house, an inexplicable, heartbreaking hate. She had not learned to love her parents, who had done nothing to earn her love. But, at least, she had always shown them respect and obedience. Why had they never returned her respect?

Annette daydreamed as she looked out at Lake Timiskaming, visible in flashes between the trees that were speeding by the window. In her mind's eye was the face of a certain handsome young man: Gérard. She had fallen in love totally unexpectedly.

Cécile and Yvonne had met Gérard, a student at Collège de Saint-Laurent, when he'd come to the hospital to see

220

his brother, who had had his appendix out. His older sister had worked as a cook and home-economics teacher at Villa Notre-Dame, and his younger sister had been the quintuplets' classmate there. Thinking that Gérard would be a good match for Annette, Cécile had decided to set them up. "Go to the waiting room," she'd told Annette. "Someone is expecting you." And that was how Annette had found herself alone with a strange young man. She'd been furious at Cécile for tricking her and had stood near the door, wanting to flee.

"Are you scared to be alone with a man?" he had asked her.

"What would you like me to say?"

"Don't you want to sit down?"

"No, thank you."

That had been the extent of their first conversation. Annette had not felt at her most attractive in her everyday clothes, especially because a seam in her skirt had given way and the split would show if she sat down. Luckily, Cécile and Yvonne had arrived, putting an end to this awkward encounter. But she and Gérard had seen each other again, and their friendship had grown into love. When they exchanged photographs, Annette wrote "Yours faithfully" on the back of hers.

Since then, the world had become an enchanted place for Annette, and she saw life with new eyes. Though she had always wanted to forget the past and had held on to only a few souvenirs of her childhood, she now treasured the memory of the tiniest details of the time she spent with Gérard, of his face, and of their favorite places. They often went out with Cécile and Laurent, and sometimes Yvonne joined them. On Gérard's arm, Annette felt taller, more womanly.

221

"The heart that sighs has not what it desires!"

Annette jumped at the sound of Yvonne's voice. She turned toward her sisters, who smiled at her tenderly.

"Does it show that much?" she asked anxiously.

"Well," Cécile joked, "your feet aren't touching the ground!"

"I'll be careful," Annette promised, to herself more than to her sisters. "They mustn't notice."

Their parents had no idea that Cécile and Annette were involved with young men. No doubt they would react badly when they found out. Their father had once taken them to see the film *The Heiress*, in which Olivia de Havilland was almost stripped of her wealth by a ne'er-do-well, and he hadn't failed to draw the moral for his daughters: rich girls must be suspicious of fortune-hunters. With his pathological mistrust of strangers, Oliva would immediately see Laurent and Gérard this way; he wouldn't bother to meet them first.

"Yes, better not to mention his name," Cécile agreed. "We'll say as little as possible, no more than we've written in our letters."

At the North Bay train station, the quints saw the front page of the latest edition of the *Nugget*. There was yet another article about them, and they scanned it quickly. Now, their father was saying that they had already signed the agreement! "I've always done my best for them," he added. "I wonder how many people realize that. Not many, I believe. All we want is for them to be happy. I've refused dozens of offers of public appearances on their behalf, all of them very lucrative. With all the adulation that surrounds the quintuplets, they could easily have thought they were better than other people." This statement, which seemed so eminently sensible, concealed a

222

message decipherable only to the members of the immediate family.

"'Better than other people!'" Yvonne muttered through clenched teeth. "I've always seen myself more like a servant."

"Let's act as if we haven't seen the *Nugget*," Cécile suggested. "Let's try to forget about the past. This visit is just a formality, a digression. Our real life is in Montreal."

Annette, who had just called home to say that they had arrived, looked worried.

"What if they don't let us leave?"

"Come on!" Yvonne protested. "We turn twenty-one today. We're adults. They can't keep us against our will."

"It's not them I'm scared of — it's me. I'm afraid I won't be able to leave. I thought I was free and strong. I have Gérard, Montreal, school. But when I hear Mom's voice, I still feel like I could crumble. Look what happened to Marie."

"We'll support each other," Cécile told her. "And we'll convince Marie to leave with us."

It was four in the morning, just about the time of day when they had been born, when their taxi stopped at the big house. The sky was already starting to get light, and the black of the night was fading into violet shadows. The buildings of Quintland looked ghostly, and the big house had never seemed more austere and closed.

But what struck them the most was to see goats grazing where the horseshoe-shaped observation gallery had been. The building had been demolished, and the wood had been sent to Espanola to build a house for Simone. The Dafoe Hospital and Nursery had been turned into a cloister for the nuns of the Order of Jesus and Mary.

"The fences!" Annette exclaimed. "Look, they're gone!"

223

The quints couldn't believe their eyes. For so many years, the chain-link fences topped with barbed wire had been their only horizon, the borders of their world.

"It's a positive sign," Cécile said, "a symbol. We're finally free!"

Once inside the house, however, she wasn't so certain. She was genuinely happy to see her parents and younger brothers, but each time one of them opened their mouth, a great apprehension took hold of her. It was as though a sort of sadness emanated from the walls of the house, perhaps because this was where she and her sisters had been so unhappy for so many years. Since most of the children had left, the family home seemed even bigger, emptier, and colder. And to think that Marie was living under this roof . . .

The sight of Marie, as submissive and constrained as they had all been as teenagers, broke her sisters' hearts. As the only daughter still at home, she had become a combination of servant, cleaning woman, and cook's helper.

"Celebrating five birthdays on the same day has always been too much trouble," Elzire said wearily. She went up to her bedroom.

Marie hastened to repair the gaffe. "I helped Mom make four cakes," she said, with unconvincing enthusiasm.

Annette wanted to answer, "And I found a boyfriend." She felt as though the last seven months had opened a deep chasm between them. It was as though Marie had remained on the shore while the others had struck out for new territories.

After breakfast, the sisters were driven to the cemetery to place flowers on Émilie's grave. They stood in a row before the gravestone for a long time, their tears flowing

224

silently. Their grief had receded, but it had not gone away, and not a single day passed that they didn't think of their departed sister. On the sixth day of each month, to mark the day she died, they said a mass in her memory.

"At least she died free," Cécile murmured softly.

This remark was addressed to Marie. Cécile had thought that it would be good to talk to her at Émilie's grave, almost as though all five of them were still together.

"Come back to Montreal with us, Peewee," Yvonne said.

"Mom and Dad need me."

"They can afford to hire a servant," Annette retorted.

"You're in school," Marie protested softly. "What would I do in Montreal?"

"You'd learn about life, like we are," Cécile answered.

"It feels so good to be master of your own destiny," Yvonne added.

"You've changed. I can see it in your eyes." Marie's face clouded over.

Annette took her hand. "No. We haven't changed. We're turning into ourselves."

"Me too, Netta!"

"No, Peewee. And as long as you stay here, you'll never know who you really are."

"Montreal . . ." Marie murmured, dropping her eyes and looking at the date on Émilie's gravestone: 1954. It was almost a year since she had died! Seeing her sisters again made the loss of Émilie more acute. She felt as though she were waking up, as though she had lived through the last few months as an automaton.

When they got back to the house, their father called them into his office, a room with paneled walls and an elaborate chandelier. Three men were already there waiting: a representative from the Guaranty Trust Company, the firm that was managing the quintuplets' fund; Mr. Donnely; and another lawyer, whom the quints had never seen before. It was the latter who read aloud in English the eight typed pages of the agreement. When he had finished, Oliva pointed to the four forms on the desk.

"You sign at the bottom, that's all."

The quints had not understood the jumble of legal terms.

"Can you read it to us again?" Cécile asked the lawyer.

With the consent of the others, he did so. The quints tried to make sense of the recitation of *whereas*'s.

"All right," their father said when the lawyer had finished, "are you satisfied? Now you can sign."

The quints exchanged glances. The three visitors, aware of the unspoken battle that was being waged between Oliva Dionne and his daughters, were ill at ease. The silence became oppressive.

"No," Cécile finally answered firmly. "We can't sign until we've had a good look at these documents."

Oliva could not hide his disappointment and fury, but he did not dare give his anger free rein in front of outsiders.

"In that case, it will have to wait a few days."

"Let us know when you're ready," said Mr. Donnely, taking his leave.

After this meeting, the climate in the house was stormy. When the quints blew out the candles on their birthday cakes, the fake joy around the table fooled no one. Oliva Dionne had suffered a rebuff; smoldering, he was planning his next move. Elzire repeatedly made seemingly innocuous remarks about the ingratitude of children.

226

The quints left for Montreal by train that very after-noon. The relief they felt at leaving was doubled by their happiness that Marie was with them. They didn't talk about what had taken place in their father's office. Through Cécile, they had stood up to their father, for the very first time in their lives! And the world had not fallen apart; the planet was still spinning on its axis.

On the train, the quints studied the document that they were supposed to sign. The agreement, which the first sentence qualified as "irrevocable," gave them full control of the interest on their money, but not on the capital, which would be paid to them in chunks: one when they turned thirty-one, another when they turned thirty-nine, and a last one when they turned forty-five. About one-third of the capital would remain for their children to inherit. If one of them died single, her money would go to their parents and would ultimately be shared equally among their own children. The house and the land on which it was built belonged to the quints, who granted its full and entire use to their parents until they died; for maintenance of the property, the quints would pay Oliva and Elzire $500 per month.

"This is practically a will!" Annette commented.

Cécile was thinking the same thing. "We should get some advice about this."

"We should start by talking to the priest in West-mount," Annette suggested. "He's a very educated man."

"I'll go with you," Marie said. "I'll get to know the city a bit."

Marie felt more lost the farther the train took her from the big house. However, with her sisters, she felt alive again.

"I have something to tell you about, too," Annette told her mysteriously. "Or, rather, someone . . ."

● ● ●

Annette and Cécile had been invited to dinner by a friend in Nicolet, and they took Gérard with them. The friend's family was very pleasant, and the house was soon filled with laughter. The joy that reigned in this family always amazed Annette and Cécile; the relationships seemed full of affection and respect. How wonderful it must have been to grow up in such an atmosphere of harmony!

As they were sitting down to dinner, the telephone rang.

"It's for you, Cécile. It's from the Institute."

Cécile went to the phone. Who could it be? And how did they know she was here? She was shocked to hear her mother's voice.

"Mom! Uh . . . hello."

"You don't sound very pleased to hear from me!"

"I'm just surprised. It's so unexpected. Is everything all right? What are you doing in Nicolet?"

"I have something to discuss with you."

They arranged to meet at a restaurant. There was no question of taking Gérard, who was still a secret from their mother.

As they approached the restaurant, Annette and Cécile began to walk more slowly. They couldn't believe that it was a coincidence Elzire was here, and Annette was worried that her mother had found out about Gérard.

"She wouldn't have come all the way from Ontario for that," Cécile said reassuringly. "It must be something else."

"Those damn agreements?"

"Perhaps."

They had been back from Corbeil for a week, and they still hadn't decided what to do. After studying the

228

document, the priest in Westmount had told them that it was all right for them to sign it, but they weren't convinced. The words "irrevocable agreement" continued to bother them. They had asked a notary to translate the document into French and then explain its implications, and they would have his answer soon.

Sitting in the car parked in front of the restaurant, Roger greeted them coldly. Marie was sitting in the back seat. Her "hello" was barely audible, and she didn't meet their eyes. She looked guilty. Maybe it was because she had returned to Corbeil two days after she arrived in Montreal. The others had tried their best to make sure she didn't feel alone and abandoned — the first day, Annette had taken her to dinner with Gérard, and Cécile had invited her to join her and Laurent at the movies the next day — but the bird had flown . . .

Cécile leaned toward Marie — she wanted to tell her not to worry — but Roger said, "The old lady's waiting for you!" and jerked his thumb toward the restaurant.

Annette asked how their mother had found them at Nicolet. Marie explained that she'd wanted to register at the Family Institute for a summer course. Their mother had decided to take her, and Roger had brought them in the car. They had stopped in Montreal, where Yvonne had told them that Annette and Cécile were in Nicolet.

Elzire, letting her spoon drop noisily into her coffee cup, was clearly in a rotten mood. Cutting short the greetings, she asked, "Why haven't you signed? If you're being stubborn, you will lose lots of money. For your own good and for ours, sign it now!"

"We're thinking about it," Cécile replied quietly.

Elzire gave her daughters a hard look. "After all we've done for you, the sacrifices, the deprivation," she

229

lamented. "This whole thing is making your father sick. Truly sick. I don't know when he will get better. The delay is killing him. If something happens to him before it's signed, it'll cause lots of problems for everyone. Oliva has always done his best for you five. Is this how you thank him?"

She paused to let her words sink in, then she implored again, "Why haven't you signed?"

Elzire continued to unreel her arguments, playing with her daughters' feelings. Sometimes she appealed to their pity; sometimes she tried to make them feel guilty. And it worked. Annette and Cécile soon stopped being young women with a future and once again became little girls certain that they were the cause of all their family's unhappiness and ashamed of having been born five at a time.

"Very well," Cécile finally conceded. "I'll sign."

Annette agreed too. Now she understood Marie's behavior, her flight from Montreal, the fact that she had already signed the agreement.

Elzire insisted on taking them back to Montreal, where the three copies of the agreement were, so that things could be settled immediately. Cécile and Annette could not refuse; Gérard would have to get home by himself.

Annette and Cécile sat on either side of Marie in the back of the car. Getting in beside Roger, Elzire said to him, "All this childishness is over. The little girls will all sign."

"And none too soon!"

Marie looked questioningly at Annette and Cécile. They nodded, and she seemed relieved.

"I've registered at the agriculture school for a summer course," Marie said.

"That's nice," Cécile answered. Her voice was neutral, but she discreetly squeezed Marie's hand to let her know how happy she was. It didn't matter where she went, as long as she got out of the big house. The agriculture school, also directed by the Sisters of the Assumption, was right beside the Family Institute; Marie would be in familiar territory.

"Will you come and see me, Cis?"

"Of course, Peewee."

"And you, Netta?"

Before Annette could answer, Elzire snapped, without turning around, "Would you stop using those stupid nicknames? You're not fifteen years old any more!"

The quints fell silent, but their eyes expressed their joy at seeing each other again.

In truth, Annette didn't really know what to say to her sister. Summer was coming, the college would close for vacation, and she would have nowhere to go except the family home in Corbeil. The prospect of being far away from her sisters, alone with her parents, was not very attractive.

After dropping Marie at the Institute, the car headed for Montreal in silence.

Yvonne joined her mother and sisters in the parking lot beside the nurses' residence. Seeing her white uniform, Elzire let out a groan.

Since Marie had already signed and the two others were ready to do so, Yvonne dropped her reservations. In the declining light of evening, the sisters signed the documents, using the hood of Roger's car as a desk.

As soon as the formalities were concluded, Elzire left. The quints stood silently, feeling sheepish. Everything had happened so fast! Their hands had been forced with completely irrational arguments.

"I have a feeling they've taken us for a ride," Yvonne muttered as her brother's car turned the corner.

• • •

On June 18, Annette got off the train at North Bay. The night before, Yvonne, Cécile, Gérard, and Laurent had driven her to the train station in Montreal. Their farewells had been sad: it would be almost three months before she'd get another chance to see the people who were dearest to her. As she had kissed her goodbye, Cécile had murmured in Annette's ear, "Don't let them get to you!"

Although Annette had told her mother when she would arrive, no one was waiting on the platform or inside the station, so she took a taxi to Corbeil. In the oppressive heat, nature seemed to be sleeping; Quintland was deserted. The taxi left, and she stood in the driveway, suitcase in hand. A sudden wave of exhaustion swept away her courage to climb the steps. A door opening in welcome or a silhouette in the window waving hello would have been enough to pull her from her lethargy. But there was no sign of life in the house or around it, nothing but a crushing silence unbroken even by bird-song or a cow mooing.

Finally, the heat of the sun drove her inside. Not daring to use the front entrance, she went around to the kitchen door. The air was completely still, and yet she felt as though she were walking into a strong head wind. She shivered. Memories came flooding into her mind about the big brick house where she had never felt at home, the prison she had so often dreamt of escaping. Among the chores, the quarrels, and the fights, there had certainly been laughter, and joy, but the periods of misery had

232

been so intense that they blocked out all the rest.

How could she have returned here of her own will? At the door she hesitated, then stopped. Minutes passed as she wondered if she should not just turn around and take the train back to Montreal without even saying hello to her family. If only it weren't so far to walk to town . . . The more time ticked by, the more her will faded. Imperceptibly, her shoulders collapsed, her spine curved, the air went out of her lungs. Should she knock? No, that would mean admitting that she felt like a stranger in this place.

Her parents' attitude toward her had changed little. Their tone was less authoritarian, but their cruelties were more insidious — and no less effective. Even their looks were full of reproach, and Annette could not help but feel at fault. No doubt because she had been away for so long, she noticed that her father had aged. His face, once narrow, had broadened, and wrinkles now crisscrossed his brow. His eyes had lost their liveliness and pride, and they held a look of defeat.

Any hopes that Annette had had for a rapprochement with Elzire were quickly snuffed out; neither tender gesture nor affectionate word was forthcoming. And to think that some of her friends liked her mother! Elzire complained and cried even more than she had before, never missing an opportunity to criticize Annette or her absent sisters. Annette's conversations with her and Oliva were limited to banal topics such as the weather. There was no question of her telling them about her adorable boyfriend, whom her sisters loved as a big brother. She missed him terribly.

To escape the tense, stifling atmosphere in the house, Annette stayed outdoors as much as possible. She worked in the garden and the fields and tended Émilie's grave, which had been quite neglected: no flowers adorned the plot, and the grass was overgrown. She quickly lost count of the days and began to feel as though she were caught up in a dream without end. Her desire for independence dissolved and she abandoned herself to her fate; the pain of being separated from her sisters was all she had left to remind her that she had another life. It was only when she read their letters or heard their voices on the telephone, especially when they gave her news of Gérard, that she would wake from her somnambulant state.

Weaving its way through the interminable, forgettable daydreams was one pressing question: *What will I do when I leave here?* She could not make a living from her love of music. Since the spring, she had been toying with the idea of becoming a nurse. Like her sisters, she felt the need to return to the millions of unknown people who had prayed and hoped for the quintuplets the love that they had shown.

Before leaving Montreal, Annette had applied to the nursing school, and she had been accepted. She had told her mother about her plans, and Elzire had refused to believe it. Two nurses in the family was enough — in fact, it was two too many! Elzire had the feeling that, subconsciously, the quints wanted to be like the women who had nurtured them after they had been torn away from her, their real mother. And she knew all the stories about what went on between doctors and nurses!

Elzire was so passionately opposed to Annette's plan, and argued her point with such vehemence, that the young woman ended up capitulating. But there was no question of her staying in Corbeil. So she registered at the

Family Institute in Nicolet, a familiar and friendly place, to study teaching and psychology. On September 6, she left for Montreal, where Yvonne and Cécile were starting their second year as student nurses, and where she would see Gérard. Being apart from him had only intensified her love.

Annette arrived in Nicolet just in time to cross paths with Marie, who was on her way to Quebec City. Having regained her strength over a peaceful summer, Marie had obtained permission to return to the convent of the Servants of the Very Holy Sacrament.

"You see, Netta? I've taken up where I left off: a novice. I don't have to go back to being a postulant!"

Although she doubted her sister's capacity to bear the hard life of the cloister, Annette did not try to keep her from going back. There was such conviction in Marie's voice, such joy in her face, such fire in her eyes, that Annette could almost believe she would triumph over her physical limitations.

"Just the thought of going back to my convent makes me feel reborn, Netta," Marie said enthusiastically. "It is my path."

• • •

In the basement of the Institute, Annette rummaged angrily through her locker. "How did *I* get stuck with this?" she grumbled as she looked for her winter coat.

An envelope fell out of her uniform pocket. It contained a letter from the mother superior of the Servants of the Very Holy Sacrament asking her to go see Marie, who had fallen ill again, and tell her that the community would not take her back when she got out of the hospital! How would Annette tell her beloved sister that she

235

couldn't fulfil her dream? It was just over a week ago that Annette had gone to Quebec City with Gérard and Cécile. Marie had been sick but was on the road to recovery, and she had described the infinite happiness that she felt within the walls of the cloister.

Suddenly, Annette heard a rumbling that seemed to rise from the cement floor. The noise became a deafening roar; the walls trembled, and she was sure that they were about to fall in upon her. Was it an earthquake? The end of the world? Her ears ringing, surprised that she was still alive, Annette rushed up the stairs to the ground floor. The vibrations had stopped and the shaking had ended. Panicked girls were screaming and nuns were running in all directions.

Outside, everything was chaos. Houses were in ruins. There were fires, clouds of dust and smoke, frightened people fleeing: it looked as if a bomb had fallen.

In fact, there had been a landslide, and part of the town had slid into the Nicolet River. The school of the Christian Brothers had collapsed and the episcopal palace had been cut in two, like a log split by an axe. The bridge was damaged, and deep cracks zigzagged along the walls of the cathedral. The telephones weren't working, and there was no public transit. The police were overseeing the evacuation of the Institute and most of the houses in town.

Not knowing where to go, Annette decided to leave Nicolet. She walked across town, collecting messages from friends who had asked her to reassure their parents. Debris and fallen telephone poles blocked the streets, and people were standing out in the open, paralyzed with fear. Firemen were trying to extinguish the fires that had burst out everywhere.

236

Annette had just one thought in mind: to get to Gérard, who was visiting his parents in Drummondville for the weekend. Hitchhiking was the only way to get there. She arrived at Gérard's home at suppertime, exhausted and covered with dust, still in a state of shock.

"I have to go to Quebec City," she told him.

"First of all, you have to calm down and rest," he replied gently.

Gérard had heard about the landslide on the radio. Worried, he had been planning to go to Nicolet, even though the authorities had told people to stay away.

Once she was with him, Annette felt better. She ate supper with his family, then wrote her parents to tell them that she had managed to escape the disaster and was staying in Drummondville "with the family of a friend." One of Gérard's friends drove them to Montreal, where Annette telephoned the parents of her friends who had asked her to give them messages. She spent the night at the nurses' residence with Cécile and Yvonne, and then took the train to Quebec City.

Marie had been hospitalized due to angina attacks. Although her face was deathly pale, she found the strength to smile at Annette and ask about what had happened in Nicolet.

"That can wait," Annette replied. "First of all, tell me how you're feeling."

"Better, much better. In fact, you almost missed me: the doctor was about to discharge me. If you have the time, you can take me back to the cloister."

"I have all the time in the world," Annette said evasively. "I'll help you pack your suitcase."

"A cloistered nun has no possessions. You know that, Netta. All my things fit in a handbag." She pointed to the folded bag sitting on her night table.

Annette sat down in the forest-green chair next to Marie's bed and took her hand. How would she tell her? She had wrestled with this question and had found no way to sugarcoat the pill. Marie asked about Yvonne, Cécile, and Gérard, and Annette gave long answers, thankful for one last respite. Then, she had to fulfil her mission.

"This is very hard to say . . ."

"What is it?"

Marie did not seem anxious, simply curious. Annette took a deep breath, then dove right in.

"I received a letter from your mother superior. Because of your health, the community cannot take you back."

Marie's features froze in total astonishment. Annette held her hand more tightly and continued. "The life is too hard on you, the mother superior said. She also believes that it is too difficult for you to be cut off from us."

"It's true that I suffer," Marie cried, devastated, "but that's *my* suffering! I offer it to God . . ." She began to sob.

Annette sat on the bed, hugged her sister, and cried with her. Rocking her head, she murmured, "You're not alone, Peewee. I'm here. Ivy and Cis, too."

After five minutes, Marie found the strength to hiccup, "What will . . . what will I do?"

"We'll take care of you."

"*What will I do?*" Marie repeated.

"It's God's will. He must have other plans for you. It's up to you to find out what they are."

The reference to divine providence calmed Marie a little bit. She thought for a moment, then said, "It's a terrible test He is sending me. I was so sure the cloister was where I belonged."

"The good Lord knows better than you, don't you think?"

Marie dried her eyes and composed herself. "Where will I go?" she asked softly.

"You mustn't go home to Corbeil."

"I don't want to, but . . ."

"Come back to Montreal with me."

"I don't have the courage to take the train, Netta."

"We'll drive in a taxi. I have enough money on me. And you know what? We'll get an apartment together in Montreal. With our monthly allowance, we'll have enough money."

Marie's face lit up a little, and then clouded over just as quickly. "What about school, Netta?"

"I don't know when they'll start again, if they ever do. They had to evacuate the Institute. We'll get a place not too far from the hospital, to be close to Yvonne and Cécile."

Annette's enthusiasm was making Marie dizzy; everything was going too quickly. Things couldn't be this simple.

"I can't leave the cloister just like that. There must be some formalities. I'll have to talk to the mother superior."

"We'll go there to pick up your things. The mother superior told me you're relieved of your vows. That means you can have your share of the trust. It seems to be very simple, and it's all taken care of."

The two sisters looked at each other with some incredulity, suddenly realizing that their lives had taken an unpredicted turn. Changing everything around in just a few minutes — this wasn't like them at all!

"Together, we'll figure it out!" Annette said.

They would have to get along all by themselves in a big city, going even farther down the road to independence than Cécile and Yvonne, who were still surrounded by rules and teachers. Would they know what to do with their freedom?

• • •

"Home sweet home!" Yvonne exclaimed as she and Cécile walked into Marie and Annette's furnished apartment in the Montreal suburb of Côte Saint-Luc for the first time.

"That's absolutely right," Marie answered, giving Yvonne a hug. "This is as much your home as ours."

"There's always room for you to stay over whenever you want," Annette added.

"Well, you'll be seeing a lot of us here!" Cécile said, gazing around the apartment. It still had an impersonal feeling, since the furnishings were the landlord's, but for the first time in her life, she was someplace where she wasn't a stranger passing through. This would be a home for all four of them!

"This is for you two, from us two," she said, holding out a gift-wrapped box.

Marie and Annette opened the gift together. It was a beautiful tablecloth with eight matching cloth napkins.

"Let's use them right away!" Annette said. "We'll set the table again."

"There's lots of time," Marie said, heading for the kitchenette. "Dinner isn't quite ready."

"I'll give you a hand," Yvonne said, following her sister.

The other two began changing the table. They spoke softly, so that Marie wouldn't hear them.

"It's wonderful to see Peewee," Cécile said. "She looks like a new person! Last week, when she arrived . . ."

"She might be the smallest one of us, but she has the most energy and willpower."

240

"Yes, but I never thought she would bounce back so quickly. They almost destroyed her in those eight months at home . . ."

"Are you whispering about me, by any chance?" Marie had come into the room without them noticing.

Her sisters had almost forgotten her teasing tone. Cécile smiled. "Yes we were talking about you, Peewee. You were so unhappy to leave the cloister. And just one week later, I find my beautiful Marie. I'm thrilled that you recovered so quickly."

Marie put the soup tureen in the center of the table. "I see it another way, Cis. We have to trust in divine providence. I wanted to pray day and night for the entire world. No doubt, that was too ambitious. I think God wants me in the world to do good things for others, to spread joy around me. Like you and Ivy are trying to do."

At dinner, the conversation was animated, personal, and wide-ranging. They were comfortable in this apartment, which Yvonne had nicknamed their "secret hideout." No one knew they were here except a few trusted and discreet friends. So that Marie and Annette would not be bothered by muckraking reporters, the telephone was registered under the name of a colleague of Yvonne and Cécile's.

"I haven't been so happy in a long time!" Yvonne exclaimed, looking merrily at her sisters. "If only Émilie were here, my joy would be complete."

"She *is* here," Marie answered. "She sees us, and she's rejoicing, too."

For a few minutes, each thought about their absent sister. These memories no longer brought the pain that they had at the beginning, but simply a feeling of loss, a nostalgia that made even more precious the inexplicable happiness that they were feeling this evening.

Yvonne and Cécile went to the apartment in Côte Saint-Luc whenever they had time off from their nursing duties. There, they recreated the sense of family that they had had at The Dafoe Hospital and Nursery. Their new home was open to their close friends: Gérard, Laurent, and some old college classmates. Yvonne and Cécile sometimes organized small parties there. Annette and Marie still hadn't bought any furniture, but they had added personal touches: piles of records, magazines, and books on the floor, clothing thrown over backs of chairs, nylons drying in the bathroom, and photographs on the walls.

Marie and Annette spent their time exploring Montreal, where they discovered a life very different from the one they had known up to now. Since there were only two of them, no one associated them with the Dionne quintuplets; the crowds on the streets thus offered a complete anonymity. No longer the objects of attention, they could observe people at their leisure, study their behavior, and learn city ways.

As they wandered, Marie was always on the lookout for a sign telling her what she should do with her life. She had accepted the fact that a cloistered existence was not for her, and that she had latched onto the notion of a religious vocation because she saw it as the only way out of the big house. Now that she saw what the world had to offer her, full of opportunities to help others and grow, her departure from the cloister no longer seemed like a rejection. The convent of the Servants of the Very Holy Sacrament must have been a step on the way to something else.

After two weeks, Annette had to return to Nicolet, where classes were starting again, even though the Institute was only half full and the town was under reconstruction. Her mind was at peace, since Yvonne and Cécile would take care of Marie — who, in any case, was beginning to take to the city like a fish to water. And Annette would be back in a few weeks for Christmas vacation. This would be her first Christmas with her only true family! No photographs for the newspapers, no forced smiles, no quarrels, no tension, only peace, tranquillity, happiness, and privacy.

• • •

Christmas ended up being far from the holiday the quints had dreamed of. Marie and Annette were patients at the hospital where their sisters worked, the former with anemia, the latter with back pain. Luckily, they were released on Christmas Eve, and the four sisters were able to celebrate Christmas together in the calm of their apartment, surrounded by close friends. Yvonne, who was not known for being emotional, declared, "This is the most beautiful Christmas of my life."

Cécile looked tenderly at Laurent. He had shocked her by proposing marriage, but more and more she was getting used to the idea that she had a right to happiness, and the idea now frightened her a little less. The desire to have children was also growing in her; more and more, she wanted to bestow upon tiny beings the love that had always been denied her.

Cécile's glance did not escape her sisters' notice. They smiled. Marie lifted her glass. "To friendship and the joy of being with people we love! I'm lucky to have sisters like you and true friends whom I love as brothers."

Marie was as generous in words as she was in deeds. This speech, in addition to the lavish gifts she had earlier given, made the others blush with embarrassment.

Two days later, however, the festive atmosphere in the apartment came to an abrupt end. With a knock on the door, their entire past came flooding in on them. Solange, a classmate of Cécile and Yvonne's, who had become a friend of all the sisters, answered.

"Hello. I'm a reporter for the *Petit Journal* and I would like to talk to the Dionne ladies."

Solange tried to close the door, but the reporter stuck his foot in it.

"You've made a mistake," she replied. "I don't know them."

It was too late. He had spotted Annette, Cécile, and Marie in the living room.

"How do you answer your father's accusations?" he shouted. "Who are the 'outsiders' who are distancing you from your family? Why didn't you go to Corbeil for the holidays?"

"Leave us alone!" Solange replied, raising her voice.

"I'm not talking to you. Are you Marie? Why aren't you at that convent in Quebec City? And where's Yvonne?"

Hearing loud voices, the superintendent came and chased away the intruder.

"I'm sorry," he said when he came back. "I didn't tell anyone you're living here. I promised to keep my mouth shut, and I did."

"We don't doubt you, Mr. Charles," Cécile reassured him.

"That's good, because . . ."

He went over to the window, parted the curtain, and pointed to a silhouette in a lighted window in the building across the way.

"I rented that apartment this morning. I think it's another reporter. He can see you from over there. Keep your curtains closed." He let the curtains fall shut and sighed. "They're real scum. I wonder who told them."

"I wonder, too," Annette retorted acerbically.

When she didn't continue he concluded, "In any case, it's someone who wanted to make trouble for you!"

Just before closing the door, he said, "Oh! I forgot. There are ten more reporters standing guard in front of the building. I didn't let them in, but if you go out . . ." And then he added, "If I can be of any help, don't be shy."

When they were alone, Marie, Cécile, and Annette looked at each other, perplexed. Had someone at the hospital revealed the location of their apartment? It wasn't impossible, but it wasn't likely.

"Will it never end?" Annette complained. "All I want is some peace!"

"This is just like Dad," Cécile said. "Reporters always call him before Christmas to find out how the quintuplets are going to spend the holidays."

Marie and Annette agreed with her. They tried to figure out the reason, but it was as impossible as ever to guess their father's motivations.

A few minutes later, Yvonne called them from work. Reporters had ferreted her out at the hospital and were asking why she and her sisters hadn't sent a Christmas card to their parents. She had protested, holding back tears, "That's not true! We sent a card a few days before Christmas. It's not our fault if it didn't arrive in time." The reporters peppered her with questions, suggesting that a "crisis" was dividing the Dionne family.

Cécile's concerns were confirmed soon after when Laurent, who had managed to elude the reporters by using a back door to the building, arrived with an armful of newspapers. The "Dionne affair" was in the headlines. Articles quoted their father's complaints that his

245

quintuplets had never sent a Christmas card or called. "We weren't surprised that the quintuplets didn't come home for the holidays," he'd said. "For some months, we've been aware that they are drawing away from us. Mrs. Dionne and I know that outsiders are to blame for this." He'd then said that he knew who these outsiders were, but he refused to identify them publicly.

He also stated, "Lately, the quintuplets have been treating their brothers and sisters with contempt. Many people have asked me why they didn't come home for the holidays. They find this strange, and they are right. Mrs. Dionne and I have thought about this for a long time, and we believe it is preferable to stop trying to hide a situation that has lasted for quite a while and is getting worse. For a number of years, we have thought that people outside the family were trying to influence the quintuplets. This was confirmed by the quints' attitude toward us since they left the house, and especially since they turned twenty-one and took possession of their money."

"The only way he would have been happy," Marie raged, covering her anguish, "would have been to keep us behind fences our whole lives, like sheep!"

Cécile said nothing. The harshness of her thoughts frightened her. She was furious at her father for venting his spleen in the newspapers. He had known perfectly well that it would upset them.

One month before, Elzire had come to have her legs examined at the hospital. Cécile had taken care of her mother while she was in Montreal, and for the first time in her life, she'd felt that Elzire was opening her heart and sharing her maternal feelings. All four had hoped against hope that their mother had finally begun to love them. Annette had even introduced her to Gérard! Elzire had promised not to tell Oliva about the existence of Annette's boyfriend, so that Annette could announce the news when she was ready. Obviously, Elzire hadn't kept her word. Cécile knew her father well enough to decode his insinuations, and she was glad she'd kept quiet about Laurent!

"He'll never leave us alone," Marie said. "He'll never take our side."

"This has got to stop!" Cécile said. "Things can't go on like this. Let's go to Corbeil and straighten it out."

"Are you serious?" Annette was stunned.

"Do I look like I'm laughing, Netta?"

"No, and it makes me nervous. Don't you think we should let the fire go out by itself?"

But Cécile had made up her mind. "If we let this pass, Marie will be right. He will never leave us in peace. Yvonne has a day off tomorrow, and I think she'll go, too."

"I don't feel well enough to make the trip," Marie said piteously.

Cécile patted her shoulder. "I know, Peewee. Maybe Solange will stay with you while we're away."

Solange agreed immediately. She had stayed out of the discussion, but now she said that she agreed with Cécile.

"I'll go with you," Annette said, "but don't count on me to say too much. I would feel better if there were someone else with us."

"You mean, an 'outsider'?" Annette asked, smiling.

"I work tomorrow," Laurent said hastily.

"Why not Gérard," Cécile suggested, "since Dad has already heard about him?"

This was precisely what Annette was thinking.

When she called him, Gérard agreed immediately.

Cécile then called Roger at work. He consented to drive them to Corbeil.

Now, they had to find a way to leave without alerting the reporters. They sketched out plans, each more far-fetched than the last. Finally, it was the superintendent who came up with the solution: they would go down to the garage in the basement and hide in the bottom of his car. He would spirit them out right under the noses of the reporters waiting out front.

Larry Edwards, the manager of the Montreal branch of the Guaranty Trust Company, agreed to help, even though he felt that they should not be going to Corbeil. Gérard and Roger would meet Yvonne, Annette, and Cécile at his house.

The ruse worked, and the quints left their building without raising any suspicions. However, another gang of reporters had guessed where they were going and were waiting for them in front of the Edwards' house. Their arms loaded with gifts for their family, they made a quick exit through the back door, which let onto the alley where Roger's car was parked.

"It's like a spy movie!" Gérard said with a smile.

"I could do without it," Yvonne grumbled. She was exhausted from work and found the prospect of a surprise visit to Corbeil depressing. It would certainly unearth memories of a past that she had done her best to bury, and she doubted that it would make things any better.

Wet snow was falling, reducing visibility and making the roads slippery, and Roger was driving fast. Yvonne dozed, leaning on Annette's shoulder, who was herself sleeping on Gérard's shoulder. Cécile couldn't sleep. She watched the road and tried to imagine the confrontation with their parents. This time, they could not give in. She had the entire night to find the right words.

In Petawawa, halfway to Corbeil, they stopped at an all-night diner. The quints felt it would be wiser to stay in the car while Gérard and Roger went for coffee. Unfortunately, the young men stumbled upon Phyllis Griffiths, the *Toronto Telegram's* tenacious correspondent in Montreal, who had been dogging the quintuplets' footsteps for years. Anticipating the quintuplets' reaction, she had hired a chauffeur to take her and her photographer to Corbeil. She recognized Roger when he entered the diner, and she rushed outside.

Cécile had opened the window to air out the car. Phyllis Griffiths poked her head inside and peppered the quints with questions, to which they responded with vague mumbles. A lightning bolt dazzled them: the photographer had just taken a picture through one of the windows. It showed only three shapes wrapped in thick coats, three pairs of eyes swollen with fatigue. Then, the reporter and the photographer jumped into their car and sped off.

When Roger's car arrived near the family home in the early morning, a large group of reporters were standing guard in front of the gate. Among them were Phyllis Griffiths and her photographer.

"Keep going," Cécile told Roger.

They continued on to Callander, where Roger phoned the house. A brother-in-law who was visiting agreed to open the gate when they arrived so that they wouldn't have to slow down where the reporters were gathered.

As they approached the house a second time, the quints once again asked their brother to keep going. He did so, thinking it was the reporters that scared them, but the real reason was that they had not found the courage

249

to confront their father. As the car rolled toward Corbeil, they actually began to hope that they would be in an accident that would send them to the hospital. Resolve and determination were fine in Montreal, but in Quintland, their decision seemed mad. For them, this was the land of resignation and docility.

As they approached the house for the third time, they didn't say anything; they didn't want Gérard to think they were ridiculous. The car went through the crowd of reporters at full speed, sending them jumping every which way. The entire family had gotten up to greet them. It was a cool reception, but it turned glacial when they spotted the "outsider."

To break the ice, Annette led her friend over to her father. "Dad, I'd like you to meet Gérard."

In her nervousness, she had addressed her father using the familiar "*tu*" instead of the respectful "*vous*"!

"What's this I hear?" he said, irritated.

Annette tried awkwardly to repair the damage, mumbling excuses about her fatigue due to eight hours on the road and no sleep. Then she made the introductions again, in proper form this time. From the look Oliva gave him, Gérard understood that he was considered an intruder. No word of welcome was uttered.

For half an hour, they talked about the weather and inquired after each other's health. There was not a word about the "crisis" that the newspapers were talking about. The quints handed out their gifts, which relaxed the atmosphere briefly, but things quickly became strained again. Then everyone went to their rooms to get a few hours of sleep.

At breakfast, Oliva Dionne gave his usual tirade about the outsiders who had always poisoned their family life.

The allusion was clear, but Gérard prudently pretended that these words had nothing to do with him. However, he could not dodge when Oliva looked him straight in the eye and said, in a tone dripping with innuendo, "People went from room to room last night! I heard bathroom doors opening and closing."

Gérard had slept in a room separated from Annette's by a common bathroom. He replied, politely but firmly, "Come on, Mr. Dionne, do you think I would do such things? Especially under your roof? It would make more sense to wait until we were in Montreal."

Oliva wasn't used to such frankness and he didn't know how to react, so he turned to Roger and asked about his work.

The atmosphere in the house was reminiscent of the heavy air before a summer cloudburst. Gérard, who was addressed as "Mr.," took refuge in a book, while Yvonne, Annette, and Cécile found themselves with nothing to do. In this house, they, too, had become outsiders.

Just before supper, Oliva asked his three daughters to come into his office. As soon as the door was closed, he began his attack.

"What do you mean, coming here with a stranger without warning us! At Christmas, your mother and I . . ."

Cécile interrupted him. "Why did you talk to the press and start this whole affair?"

Her voice was trembling with rage, and she was as surprised as her father when the words that she had been seeking in vain since the night before came out all by themselves, as loud as thunderclaps.

"What possessed you to say all those things about us? Why are you making up stories, when we never said anything at all?"

For the first time, Oliva did not try to blame his "little girls." On the contrary, he admitted that he had made a mistake by complaining to the newspapers because of a late Christmas card.

"You're the one who makes up stories and invents 'crises,'" Cécile continued. "We've closed the door on the past. But believe me, there are things we *could* say if we wanted to."

Oliva nodded his head pitifully. He said that he had let himself be influenced by other members of the family and repeated that he had made a mistake. He almost went so far as to ask their forgiveness.

Yvonne, Annette, and Cécile couldn't believe their ears. They were as surprised by their father's words as by those that Cécile had pronounced in their name. Even yesterday, they would never have imagined that such a scene was possible, that they would have the better of this man, before whom they had once cowered. They had changed much more than they'd thought. As they left the room, each one felt that she had finally grown up.

To put an end to the newspaper articles alleging a "crisis in the Dionne family," Oliva issued a press release chalking the affair up to a simple misunderstanding, and the family posed for pictures. But the absence of smiles and the tension were there for all to see, and most reporters were not fooled. Obviously, the "misunderstanding" went deeper than Oliva claimed.

● ● ●

The quints returned to Montreal, and Annette went back to Nicolet. Marie told Yvonne and Cécile about a plan that she had been hatching for several weeks: she wanted to start a business. What she found most interesting and knew a little bit about, even if it was only as a customer, was the flower business. So she would open a flower shop!

"I don't have any experience, it's true," she told her sisters, "but I'll learn. I'll make a go of it."

This show of independence delighted her sisters. It was as if Marie were breaking an ancient curse that was still weighing upon them: *You are good for nothing, you will never be capable of doing anything.* If any one of them could prove the contrary, it was Marie. In spite of her often fragile health, she had enough determination and courage to do anything.

Evenings at the apartment in Côte Saint-Luc were soon spent drawing up plans and preparing strategies. Gérard and Laurent were also interested in Marie's project; Laurent was even considering quitting his job at Radio-Canada to help with the shop. But launching a business required capital, and although Marie had some $200,000 in her account with Guaranty Trust, she could not use this money freely. Because of the agreement the quints had signed, she could only ask the committee that managed her funds to give her the several thousand dollars she needed. Surely, they wouldn't refuse her a small percentage of her own fortune for such a worthy cause!

Marie seemed very confident about the answer from the trust company, although she still had some private doubts. The committee that controlled her money was composed of her father, her father's lawyer, and a Guaranty Trust representative. She was sure that Oliva Dionne held the balance of power. If she could win him over, the others would acquiesce.

Hoping for a lucky break, Marie went to Corbeil to explain her plans to her parents, and Laurent accompanied her. The family was still not aware of his existence, and this was not the time to introduce them to a new "outsider," so he waited in North Bay while Marie took a taxi to Corbeil. Their plan was that in one hour Laurent would take another taxi to come and get her. If she needed more time to convince her parents, she would hang a handkerchief outside the house and Laurent would understand that he should come back a bit later.

Elzire and Oliva were surprised by their daughter's unplanned visit, and their greeting, as usual, was reserved. Marie had brought orchids for her mother and a bouquet of roses to leave at Émilie's grave.

"Are you crazy?" Elzire exclaimed, fiddling distractedly with the petals of an orchid. "Putting flowers in a cemetery in the middle of winter! People will laugh at us. We'll give them to the nuns for their chapel."

Marie ignored her mother's comment and quickly mustered all her enthusiasm to describe her plan. But her parents soon began to smile sarcastically.

"Poor innocent child!" her father murmured. "You know nothing about business. It'll be a total flop."

Marie tried to prove how seriously she was approaching her flower business, but Oliva's attitude worsened. He began to shout, and harsh words were exchanged.

Elzire angrily threw the orchids to the floor. "Florist! Don't make me laugh! Why not just go ahead and be a housemaid while you're at it?"

Turning to her father, Marie implored, "Will you put in a good word for me with Guaranty Trust?"

He paused, as if he were weighing the pros and cons, but in reality he was savoring the power that he still had over his quints. Finally, he declared, in a moralistic tone, "My role is to administer your assets properly, as I have always done. And this means sometimes I have to protect you from yourself."

Marie gave up all hope, but she did not want to give them the satisfaction of seeing that she was defeated. "I have to go back to Montreal," she said. "I have lots to do if my store is going to be open for Mother's Day."

Out of the corner of her eye, she saw the five orchids scattered on the floor that she had so often washed on her hands and knees. Five delicate, precious flowers. Elzire had understood very well the symbolism of this bouquet. The broken flowers strewn on the linoleum were the very image of what their life had been, hers and her sisters', in this house. Her heart in pieces, she kept her head high.

"I have business in North Bay," Oliva said. "I'll drop you off at the train station."

As they left the house, a taxi slowed down in front of the gate. Marie quickly opened the garage door, hoping that Laurent would interpret her signal correctly. He understood. The taxi picked up speed.

At the train station, Laurent avoided looking at them, pretending to be a traveler in a rush. He and Marie got onto the same train car, but by different doors, and sat at opposite ends so that they would not arouse Oliva's suspicions. They moved together only after the train was out of the station.

As she had expected, Marie's request for funds was refused by the trust company immediately and summarily. Her father and the other two committee members no doubt thought that their decision would put an end to her project, so they were surprised when she declared proudly, "I'm going ahead with the shop. I won't stop now! I'll find the capital elsewhere."

255

The refusal only reinforced Marie's determination. She took a training course with a cousin of Gérard's who was a florist in Sorel, learning how to run a business, purchase flowers from wholesalers, keep them fresh, and arrange them attractively. When he thought she was ready, her mentor went to Montreal with her to help search out a suitable location for her shop. They found a space on the ground floor of a new building, at the corner of Pine Avenue and St. Urbain Street, near several major hospitals. Marie signed the lease and put a hand-written sign in the window: "Watch for our opening on May 10."

There wasn't much time to decorate the shop, and the money question still wasn't solved. The other quints each had several hundred dollars in their bank accounts, which they gladly lent to Marie. Then, the four sisters decided to stop the supplementary allowance they had been paying to their parents. When their mother had complained that they couldn't make ends meet on the $500 a month provided for in the agreement, the quints had asked the trust company to decrease their own monthly allowance by $300 and send this amount to their parents. Now, Marie needed it more than Elzire and Oliva did.

Even scraping the bottom of the barrel, Marie didn't have enough to pay for the furnishings and supplies for her shop. But she had an account at Eaton's, for which Guaranty Trust paid the balance every month. So, she had thirty days to acquire everything she needed. When the trust company received the bill, it would be too late; it would have to be paid! *After all, it's my money!* Marie said to herself.

Every day, she and Laurent scoured the shelves at

Eaton's to find everything she needed, from letterhead to business cards to invoices, which she had printed with the name and address of her store. Since she didn't have a car to carry all her purchases, she hired a taxi driver, who agreed to give her a bill at the end of the month. She would send it to Guaranty Trust.

Marie's sisters soon became involved in her venture. After work, Yvonne and Cécile came to the store to help, and to hear Marie's funny stories about her shopping exploits. They laughed when they thought of the look on the faces of the management committee members when they saw the bills at the end of the month.

"You should call your store 'Eaton's,'" Yvonne suggested jokingly.

Marie claimed that she had already found a name, but she didn't want to reveal it right now. "In the proper time and place," she answered when they asked her about it. "It's a surprise."

On the morning of May 19, nine days from her twenty-second birthday, Marie finally opened her store. She and Laurent had spent the entire night making the final touches, but she wasn't tired at all. On the contrary, she felt as though she was grabbing onto life with both hands and conquering the world.

Annette, who had come from Nicolet, Cécile, and Yvonne arrived half an hour before the shop opened to provide their sister with moral support and bask in the glow of her triumph. Perhaps they would draw from her example the determination to follow their own dreams.

When they saw the name of the store painted on the window, they were very moved: it was "Salon Émilie." They had speculated that Marie might include the name of their dead sister in the name of her store, but they hadn't said anything so as not to spoil her pleasure in surprising them.

"I have flowers for you," she said, "but I want to give them to you in front of the photographers."

"A true businesswoman!" Annette teased proudly.

"For once, we'll be photographed because we want to be," Yvonne said.

Marie looked at her watch. "One minute more," she said nervously.

Cécile gave her a kiss. "I haven't wished you good luck, Peewee," she murmured. "Bravo! You've proved to the world that we're not as stupid as some people said."

"Dad and Mom won't be coming," Marie said, unable to hide her disappointment. "I sent them an invitation, but they didn't even answer."

"It's just as well," Cécile answered. "They would have found a way to spoil your big day."

Marie sauntered to the door, a key-ring jingling in her right hand.

"Today, I'm giving away my flowers!"

"Don't be too generous, Marie," Gérard said. "We have to pay the wholesaler for them."

"So what! Today, I want to make people happy."

All the Montreal newspapers had sent a photographer and a reporter, and a number of correspondents from foreign newspapers had shown up as well. Without having to be asked, the quints posed together.

A young photographer from *La Presse*, on his first day on the job, was surprised when he framed the famous Dionne quints in his camera viewfinder. They didn't look at all like the photographs of them that he had seen. These young women had faces full of life, sparkling eyes, smiles that seemed to come from the heart. In their photographs, he had always seen smiles plastered on like

258

masks, and a tired look in their eyes. It was said that they ran away from reporters; he saw them answering questions simply and directly.

What had changed? The young man studied them carefully, and soon he had his answer: they didn't look so much like each other! Each had her own hairdo and her own style. In fact, they weren't at all hard to tell apart.

He then noticed the languorous glances that Cécile and Annette were casting at the two young men behind the counter. There was love in the air!

"Here."

Marie's voice made him jump. He'd been so wrapped up in his observations that he hadn't seen her coming toward him, holding out a bouquet.

"For me?"

"Yes, to thank you for coming." She had an ineffable smile, a happy look. He took the flowers and wished her success.

Yvonne had retreated to a spot near the door to admire her sisters' ease in the midst of strangers. Then she looked out the window at the hospital across the street. Its gray stones slowly faded, along with the sound of happy conversations.

She saw herself on a November evening, walking with her four sisters across a field over which an ominous wind blew. Her Shirley Temple doll under her left arm, a suitcase in her right hand, she was following her father, who was leading them to the big house like a shepherd leading his flock. It had been thirteen years, and she still had not managed to forget it completely. Suddenly, she heard a noise coming from the past, weakly at first, but getting stronger. Her father's footsteps echoing along the hallway!

She quickly turned her head and dove back into the

animated store, sweeping her memories away. Marie was ruling the roost, playing the perfect hostess, neglecting no one. Cécile and Annette had sidled over to their boyfriends. The long night that had begun in November 1943 was finally over, but, God, so many tears had been shed before morning!

Afterword

A few months after Salon Émilie opened, Marie was forced to sell her business. Not only had some employees taken advantage of her, but she was a victim of her own generosity: she gave away as many flowers as she sold.

Annette got married in October 1957, and Cécile in 1958, both to their first true loves. Also in 1958, Marie secretly married a man fourteen years her senior.

Once Yvonne finished nursing school, she turned to sculpting, and later she became a librarian.

Cécile had five children, one of whom died in infancy. Annette had three sons; Marie, two daughters. Both Marie's and Cécile's marriages lasted only six years; Annette's marriage broke up after sixteen years.

Oliva and Elzire Dionne lived in the "big house" until the early 1960s. The building was then converted to a senior citizens' home. The final break between the four surviving quintuplets and the rest of the family came in 1958. The next time they saw each other was twelve years later, at the funeral of Marie, who died of a stroke at age thirty-five. The "two families" were brought together again for the funerals of Oliva, in 1979, and Elzire, in 1986.

Although they made great efforts, repairing their damaged personalities, recapturing their self-esteem, and developing confidence in their abilities proved to be a long process. As well, Annette and Cécile were single parents, seeing to their children's education and welfare alone. Yvonne, who remained single, had the support of sincere, devoted friends.

Now in their sixties, Annette, Cécile, and Yvonne Dionne all live in the same suburb of Montreal. They have made peace with themselves and their past, and face the future with tranquillity. They hope that this book, written without bitterness, will help to bring children and teenagers the respect they deserve and be a ray of hope for all victims of injustice.